it's teatime

—let's celebake

sophia handschuh

To my lovely mum –
one of the biggest afternoon tea fans I have ever known.

First published in Great Britain
in 2017 by Sophia Handschuh
Enquiries: admin@thermomixbakingblogger.com
www.thermomixbakingblogger.com

Text © Sophia Handschuh
Copyeditor: Emma Buckley
Design © Sophia Handschuh and Jesse Sutton-Jones
Text design and typesetting by Anna Green at siulendesign.com
Photography © Sophia Handschuh

contents

introduction

—Afternoon tea is like a visit from the Queen

There is nothing more British than afternoon tea. Well, there is, but when I first came to London many years ago I discovered the world of afternoon tea. I immediately fell in love with the concept and absolutely adore the idea of having small finger sandwiches without crusts, little mini tarts, scones and a lovely cup of tea. From majestic cakes like the oriental rose cake to the most intricate finger-sized petits fours, I have structured this book to give you the best of every aspect of afternoon tea. Needless to say, there will be some traditional scones (or how do you pronounce it again?) and classic recipes such as the cherry Bakewell tart but I have also gone deep into my imagination to recreate classics and add a twist to them.

I love organising an afternoon tea party and recently, when it was my mum's birthday in December I finally decided this had to be the theme of my next book. The joy I got from making so many varied recipes and presenting them on the table for her guests was completely worth the effort for me. I had so much fun and balanced the sweet and savoury elements so well that it created a superb afternoon of indulgence. Her guests were so impressed that they asked me for the recipes and wanted to know more about afternoon tea. But to explain the art of afternoon tea, mastering the three-tiered cake stands and fine china, the perfectly decorated tables and creating an ensemble between the delicious treats and the teas that are served, I had to do some more research. After many cups of teas, I have put together a masterpiece and I am really looking forward to guiding you through this journey into afternoon tea. Perhaps this poem might explain it all:

The Tea Party

I had a little tea party
This afternoon at three.
'Twas very small–
Three guest in all–
Just I, myself and me.

Myself ate all the sandwiches,
While I drank up the tea;
'Twas also I who ate the pie
And passed the cake to me.

—Jessica Nelson North

Enjoy the book!

history

Although afternoon tea could be classed as quintessentially British, the art of drinking tea has crossed continents and centuries. Ever since the third millennium tea has been a part of Chinese culture but travelled over to England in the 1600s. It was Anna, the seventh duchess of Bedford, however who might be responsible for the uprising of afternoon tea. She always used to be hungry between 4 o' clock and dinner time which was served at 8 o'clock in her house. She would ask for a tray of tea, bread and butter and cake to be brought to her room to fill the long period between lunch and dinner. This became a habit of hers and soon she started inviting some friends to join her. Needless to say, the rest is history.

In fact, afternoon tea became so fashionable that in the 1880s upper class and high society women dressed up in their finest gowns, gloves and hats to enjoy afternoon tea in the drawing room between four and five o'clock. Traditionally, the afternoon tea serving consisted of a variety of dainty sandwiches, scones served with clotted cream and jam (it is debatable which one goes on first) and bite-sized cakes and pastries. Tea was an essential part of the ceremony and was usually Indian grown or Ceylon tea served in silver pots.

Nowadays, afternoon tea usually consists of a three-tiered stand with a very similar selection of food and is paired with Earl grey or Assam tea. Or if you are at home, teatime consists of a cup of hot tea with some biscuits for dipping. In this book I have put together a selection of teatime menus (p.10) so that you can create your own customised afternoon tea party and decide on your own dress code. It could be funny to dress up in hats and gloves – why not! But most importantly, don't forget to enjoy yourself, relax and have a lovely time with your loved ones. After all, 'There are few hours in life more agreeable than the hour dedicated to the ceremony known as afternoon tea' (Henry James).

teatime menus

—Choose your favourite

When you are planning your perfect afternoon tea party, it is always best to start by formulating your menu. I have put together some really lovely menus, sorted by occasion, that use the recipes in this book. There are so many different menus listed that I am sure you will have no trouble finding your perfect fit. Whether it is for your best friend's bridal shower or a champagne tea, these menus are designed to help you prepare for that special occasion. As a rule of thumb, I usually prepare about three to four sweet treats and one to two savoury snacks to create a well-balanced afternoon tea party. You can prepare many of these recipes in advance so you won't have to worry too much on the day, leaving you with more time to decorate and get ready!

birthday party

Raspberry Iced Buns
Mini Cinnamon Scrolls
Fragrant Rose Cake
Macadamia Brownies
Cherry Bakewell Tarts
Jammie Dodgers
Cucumber & Apple Sandwiches
Olive Anchovy Wheels

anniversary

Beetroot Cured Salmon
Savoury Eccles Cakes
Blueberry Scones
Hazelnut & Apricot Roulade
Salted Caramel Eclairs
Strawberry & Hibiscus Curd Tart
Cardamom Biscuits

father's day

Pastrami & Emmental Sandwiches
Cheesy Scones
Battenberg
Salted Caramel Eclairs
Limoncello Mini Tarts
Ginger Custard Creams

valentine's day

Beetroot Cured Salmon
Mini Lobster Rolls
Raspberry Scones
Raspberry Crème Genoise
Rhubarb Puff Tartlets
Strawberry & Prosecco Tarts
Cardamom Biscuits

bridal shower

Cucumber & Apple Sandwiches
Mini Lobster Rolls
Buttermilk Scones
Fragrant Rose Cake
Pimm's Cream Puffs
Coconut Tart
Pecan Shortbread

festive canapés

Vanilla Cured Salmon
Savoury Eccles Cakes
Gingerbread Scones
Apple & Pecan Cake
Apricot Lavender Bites
Jammy Jam Tarts
Chocolate Biscotti

baby shower

Smoked Salmon Sandwiches
Olive Anchovy Wheels
Raspberry Iced Buns
Rhubarb Cheesecake
Apricot Lavender Bites
Raspberry Almond Tart
Jammie Dodgers

mother's day

Beetroot Cured Salmon
Egg Salad Sandwiches
Blueberry Scones
Macadamia Brownies
Chocolate Mocha Tart
Passionfruit Jaffa Cakes

teatime menus *continued*

traditional tea

Smoked Salmon Sandwiches
Cucumber & Apple Sandwiches
Buttermilk Scones
Earl Grey Teacakes
Coffee & Walnut Cake
Salted Caramel Eclairs
Cherry Bakewell Tart
Ginger Custard Creams

champagne tea

Egg Salad Sandwiches
Vanilla Cured Salmon
Pumpkin Scones
Lavender Honey Cake
Pimm's Cream Puffs
Limoncello Mini Tarts
Lavender Shortbread

breakfast tea

Smoked Salmon Sandwiches
Raspberry Iced Buns
Buttermilk Scones
Apple Spiced Tea Loaf
Jammy Jam Tarts
Peanut Butter Cookies

something special

Mini Lobster Rolls
Beetroot Cured Salmon
Raspberry Scones
Raspberry Crème Genoise
Salted Caramel Eclairs
Fresh Fig Tart
Jammie Dodgers

gluten free tea

Egg Salad Sandwiches
Vanilla Cured Salmon
Black Forest Mini Gateaux
Raspberry Scones
Lemon Mascarpone Tart
Tahini Cookies
Pecan Shortbread

key to dietary labels

F	Freezable
RSF	Refined sugar free
GF	Gluten free
WF	Wheat free
DF	Dairy free
NE	No eggs
V	Vegan

sandwiches & savoury bites

gluten free sandwich bread

—So fluffy

makes
1 large
loaf

prep:
2 hrs

60g chickpea liquid (from ½ can chickpeas, keep the chickpeas refrigerated for later use)

1 tsp cream of tartar

350g water

30g maple syrup

1 Tbsp dried active yeast (or 30g fresh yeast)

380g gluten free plain flour

1 tsp xanthan gum

1 Tbsp gluten free baking powder

1 tsp sea salt

60g olive oil

10g apple cider vinegar

1. Preheat the oven to 190°C / 170°C Fan / Gas Mark 5. Line a loaf tin (1-pound) with greaseproof paper and set aside.
2. Insert the butterfly whisk. Add the chickpea liquid and cream of tartar and whisk 4 Min. / Speed 3.5. Remove and transfer into a small bowl. Set aside.
3. Remove the butterfly whisk. Add the water, maple syrup, dried active yeast, gluten free flour, xanthan gum, baking powder, sea salt, olive oil and vinegar and combine 20 Sec. / Speed 5 while helping with your spatula through the lid.
4. Add the whisked chickpea liquid and fold in using your spatula until just incorporated.
5. Pour into the prepared tin and leave to rise for 20 minutes, then bake for 60 minutes until golden brown (if crust gets too brown after 40 minutes, cover the loaf with foil). Remove and transfer onto a wire cooling rack. Leave to cool before slicing. The bread stores well in a bread bag for up to 2 days.

dark rye bread

—Moist and aromatic

makes
1 large
loaf

prep:
4 hrs

500g whole rye grains

200g carrots, in small pieces

200g soya yoghurt

200g water

1 Tbsp dried active yeast (or 30g fresh yeast)

100g sunflower seeds

2 tsp sea salt

1 tsp diastatic malt powder (optional)

60g molasses

1. Place 250g rye grains in the mixing bowl. Grind 1 Min. / Speed 10. Transfer to a separate bowl and set aside. Add the remaining rye grains to the mixing bowl and grind 25 Sec. / Speed 10. Add the carrots and blitz 5 Sec. / Speed 8.
2. Add the reserved rye flour, soya yoghurt, water, yeast, sunflower seeds, sea salt, malt powder (if using) and molasses then combine 1.5 Min. / Reverse / Speed 4.
3. Pour the mixture in a 2-pound loaf tin lined with greaseproof paper. Place in an un-preheated oven and bake at 160°C / 140°C Fan / Gas Mark 3 for 3 hours.
4. Once baked, remove from the oven and leave to cool before slicing. You can store the bread in a bread bag for up to 1 week.

sandwich bread

—White, wholemeal or spelt

makes
1 large
loaf

300g water
1 Tbsp dry active yeast (or 30g fresh yeast)
20g olive oil
10g honey

For white sandwich bread
500g strong white bread flour
1 Tbsp sea salt flakes

For wholemeal sandwich bread
500g strong wholemeal bread flour
1 Tbsp sea salt flakes

For spelt sandwich bread
250g white spelt flour
250g wholemeal spelt flour
1 Tbsp sea salt flakes

prep:
2-3 hrs

1. Place the water, dry active yeast, olive oil and honey in the mixing bowl and warm **2 Min. / 37°C / Speed 2.5.**
2. Add the flour and sea salt flakes and knead **2 Min. / Kneading Function**. Transfer to a large glass bowl and cover with cling film. Leave to rise for 1-2 hours at room temperature until doubled in size.
3. Preheat the oven to 200°C / 180°C Fan / Gas Mark 6. Line a 2-pound loaf tin with greaseproof paper.
4. Transfer the dough onto a lightly floured surface. Flatten and shape it into a rectangle the size of the tin with your fingers. Roll up lengthways and place seam side down in the prepared tin. Cover with a tea towel and leave to rise for a further 45 minutes. Place in the oven, spray water around the inside of the oven then bake for 20-25 minutes until it sounds hollow when tapped.

egg salad

—With watercress

This egg salad is one of my favourites. My partner Jesse and I are in disagreement about anything that contains boiled eggs. But that just means more for me! I have tried to uplift the traditional recipe and included some mango chutney and fresh watercress. It works so well and creates a lovely, balanced flavour.

makes
16

4 eggs
800g water
150g mayonnaise
40g mango chutney
20g Dijon mustard
½ tsp smoked paprika
1 pinch sea salt
1 pinch black pepper
8 slices white sandwich bread (p. 21)
10g fresh watercress

prep:
10 min

1. To boil the eggs, place them in the simmering basket. Fill the mixing bowl with the water and boil for **15 Min. / 100°C / Speed 1**. Drain and rinse the eggs under cold water. Leave to cool. Clean the mixing bowl.
2. Place the mayonnaise, mango chutney, mustard, smoked paprika, salt and black pepper in the mixing bowl. Combine **20 Sec. / Speed 2**.
3. Peel the eggs and add to the mixing bowl. Chop **3 Sec. / Speed 3**.
4. Place the sandwich slices on a chopping board and cut the crusts off. Spread 4 sandwich slices with the egg salad and top with some watercress. Top with the other sandwich slices and cut each in half diagonally and each of those halves in triangles. You will end up with mini bite-sized sandwiches. Serve immediately or chill until needed.

home-cured salmon

—Vanilla or beetroot

How exciting is it that you can home-cure your own salmon? I love the idea of these flavours and have developed two different cures for you to try at home. It is best to use a very fresh piece of salmon fillet from your local fishmonger.

serves
6

For the beetroot cure

200g raw beetroot, peeled and halved
1 tsp pink peppercorns
1 tsp fennel seeds
1 tsp juniper berries
60g sea salt flakes
60g raw cane sugar
1 lemon, zest only
½ orange, zest only
10g fresh dill
500g skinless, pin-boned salmon fillet
3 Tbsp vodka

For the vanilla cure

2 tsp vanilla bean paste
60g sea salt flakes
60g raw cane sugar
3 Tbsp vodka

rye bread, to serve
capers, to serve

prep:
20 min

cure:
2 days

Prepare a large rectangular tray with three layers of cling film and set aside.

For the beetroot salmon

1. Place the beetroot, peppercorns, fennel seeds, juniper berries, salt, sugar, lemon and orange zest and dill in the mixing bowl. Blitz **2 Sec. / Speed 7**. If it is not quite chopped finely, repeat.
2. Pour a third of the cure onto the prepared tray making a shape as large as the salmon fillet. Place the salmon on top and spread with the remaining cure to make an even layer. Spoon over the vodka and wrap tightly in the cling film. Place another tray on top and use something to weigh it down. Refrigerate for 2 days to cure.

For the vanilla salmon

1. Place the vanilla bean paste, salt, sugar and vodka in the mixing bowl and combine **10 Sec. / Speed 2**.
2. Pour a third of the cure on the prepared tray making a shape as large as the salmon fillet. Place the salmon on top and spread with the remaining cure to make an even layer. Wrap tightly in cling film and place another tray on top and use something to weigh it down. Refrigerate for 2 days to cure.

Remove from the fridge and rinse well. Pat dry with a kitchen towel and thinly slice the salmon. Serve with some fresh capers on rye bread.

cucumber & apple

—With zesty lemon

These tasty little cucumber and apple sandwiches are so refreshing and the perfect balance for some of the sweet treats on the table. The best thing is, they are so easy to prepare and great for the kids.

makes
16

8 slices gluten free sandwich bread (p. 20)
1 cucumber, halved and deseeded
1 apple, cored and quartered
10g lemon juice
1 tsp cider vinegar
5g chives, chopped
1 pinch sea salt
1 pinch black pepper
20g sunflower or vegetable spread

prep:
10 min

1. Cut the crusts off the sandwich bread slices. Set aside.
2. Place the cucumber, apple, lemon juice, cider vinegar, chives, salt and pepper in the mixing bowl. Chop **3 Sec. / Speed 4**. Drain away any excess juices using the simmering basket.
3. Spread each bread slice with sunflower or vegetable spread and top with some of the filling. Place another bread slice on top and cut into squares. Serve immediately or keep covered with cling film and refrigerated until serving.

Tip: Chives are best chopped by hand. Although the Thermomix is excellent at chopping most herbs, chives are slightly more tricky. I usually bundle the chives up and use kitchen scissors to cut them directly into the mixing bowl in small pieces. Much easier than chopping with a knife.

pastrami & emmental

—New York style

Recently we went to New York and what I discovered there were probably some of the best sandwiches I have ever had. I was on a mission to try the best sandwich places Manhattan had to offer and I wasn't let down. These pastrami and Emmental sandwiches are a mix of my two favourite sandwiches I had in New York delis and I think they make a gorgeous addition to an afternoon tea ceremony.

makes 8

250g white cabbage, cut in large pieces
2 carrots, in small chunks
20g cider vinegar
100g mayonnaise
20g ketchup
10g American mustard
10g caster sugar

8 slices rye bread (p. 20)
50g unsalted butter, softened
8 Emmental slices
8 pastrami slices
8 small gherkins
20g American mustard

prep: 20 min

1. To make the coleslaw, place the white cabbage, carrots, cider vinegar, mayonnaise, ketchup, American mustard and caster sugar in the mixing bowl. Blitz **3 Sec. / Speed 5**. Transfer to a bowl and set aside.
2. Spread the butter on the rye bread slices, top with some of the coleslaw, followed by a slice of Emmental, a slice of pastrami and a small gherkin. Finish off with a squeeze of American mustard on each sandwich and serve immediately or cover with cling film and chill before serving.

smoked salmon

—And chive schmear

I must admit, when I first came to the UK I was not a big fan of crustless sandwiches. I couldn't quite understand how you could do that to your lovely crust. However, Jesse introduced me to smoked salmon and cream cheese sandwiches when we were watching the tennis in the summer and I was then convinced that it is actually fine to cut off the crusts to create something so delicate and tasty. This one is my all-time favourite and the chive schmear is something I discovered in New York.

makes
16

8 slices wholemeal or spelt sandwich bread
  (p. 21)
50g unsalted butter, softened
½ lemon, zest only
2 tsp lemon juice
1 pinch sea salt
1 pinch black pepper

300g cream cheese
20g chives, chopped
400g thickly sliced, high quality smoked
  salmon

prep:
10 min

1. Cut the crusts off the bread slices and spread each slice with butter. Set aside.
2. To make the chive schmear, place the lemon zest, lemon juice, salt, pepper, cream cheese and chives in the mixing bowl. Combine **20 Sec. / Speed 2**.
3. Spread 4 sandwich slices with the chive schmear and top with some salmon. Sandwich the slices together with the remaining bread and cut in half diagonally. You can cut them in half again to make triangles or leave them as they are. Serve immediately or cover with cling film and chill before serving.

olive anchovy wheels

—The perfect balancing act

Afternoon tea is not just about sweets. My partner Jesse is completely obsessed with anchovies and recently we discovered a new fishmonger around the corner from our flat in London. He sells by far the best tasting anchovies I've ever had and I immediately went on to develop a recipe for them. These olive anchovy wheels are a perfect little bite to have when you feel like you've had a few too many sweets. They will balance your tastebuds and prepare you for more.

makes
6

250g plain flour + extra for dusting
150g water
250g block of butter

70g black olives
30g anchovy fillets in oil

1 garlic clove, peeled
5g fresh parsley
1 pinch black pepper
20g olive oil

prep:
2 hrs

1. To make the pastry, place the plain flour and water in the mixing bowl. Mix **20 Sec. / Speed 6.** Transfer to a bowl and cover with cling film. Refrigerate for 2 hours.

2. Put the block of butter between two sheets of greaseproof paper. Using a rolling pin, roll it into a 15cm square, keeping the edges straight. Leave wrapped in the greaseproof paper and chill for 30 minutes. On a lightly floured surface, roll out the dough to a 30cm x 30cm square. Place the butter on top at a 45° angle so that one edge of the butter is facing you.

3. Fold over each corner of the dough to the centre to make a parcel. Use a pastry brush to brush off any excess flour. Press down the edges and flip upside down. Wrap in cling film and freeze for 10 minutes.

4. Once chilled, unwrap and roll out the dough to a rectangle of 20cm x 50cm. Roll out gently – do not press too hard, otherwise the butter will split. Fold the bottom third up, making sure that you keep brushing off the excess flour. Fold the top third down so that the dough is folded up like a letter. Wrap in cling film and freeze for 10 minutes. This is called a turn.

5. Remove from the freezer, unwrap and place the dough in front of you so that the folded edge faces your right. Repeat the same rolling out, folding, freezing process another three times. Preheat the oven to 200°C / 180°C Fan / Gas Mark 6. Line a large rectangular baking tray with greaseproof paper and set aside. Clean the mixing bowl.

6. Place the black olives, anchovy fillets, garlic clove, parsley, black pepper and olive oil in the mixing bowl and blitz **2 Sec. / Speed 7.** Scrape down using spatula. Repeat this step 3-4 times until the mixture is finely chopped.

7. Roll out the pastry into a long thin rectangle approx. 20cm x 40cm. Spread the filling mixture over the pastry evenly. Roll up starting from one short end into a tight log. Wrap in cling film and freeze for 10 minutes.

8. Cut up into ½cm thick pieces and place them on the prepared trays, leaving some space in between each wheel. Bake in the oven for 10 minutes until golden brown. Remove and transfer onto a wire cooling rack. Leave to cool before serving.

mini lobster rolls

—So buttery

What a treat! I love lobster rolls and when I first tried them in London a few years back, I fell in love with the taste and texture. If you are in a hurry you can buy hot dog buns, but there is nothing better than making them yourself at home. It is super fast.

makes 12

150g whole milk
150g water
1 Tbsp dried active yeast (or 30g fresh yeast)
20g caster sugar
500g strong white bread flour
30g unsalted butter, in small cubes
10g sea salt

90g unsalted butter

15g dill
1 celery stick, in large chunks
10g chives, chopped
450g cooked lobster meat (from a large 1.2kg lobster)
½ lemon, juice only
1 pinch sea salt
1 pinch black pepper

prep: 2-3 hrs

1. To make the rolls, place the milk, water, yeast and sugar in the mixing bowl. Warm **2 Min. / 37°C / Speed 2.5**. Add the flour, butter and salt and knead **2 Min. / Kneading Function**. Transfer to a large bowl and cover with cling film. Leave to rise for 1-2 hours at room temperature until doubled in size.

2. Tip the dough onto a floured surface, cut into 12 pieces and roll each piece into a long log approx. 15cm. Place them very close to each other on a large rectangular baking tray lined with greaseproof paper. Cover with a tea towel and leave to rise for another hour. Meanwhile, preheat the oven to 200°C / 180°C Fan / Gas Mark 6.

3. Uncover the hot dogs and place them in the oven. Spray water around the inside of the oven then bake for 15 minutes until golden brown but still soft. Remove and transfer onto a wire cooling rack. Leave to cool.

4. Meanwhile, to make the lobster filling, place the dill in the mixing bowl. Chop **2 Sec. / Speed 7**. Scrape down, then add the celery stick and chop **2 Sec. / Speed 5**. Scrape down and add the chives, lobster, lemon juice, salt and pepper. Chop **2 Sec. / Speed 4**.

5. Cut each cooled hot dog bun in half and slice each half open vertically. Melt the butter in a large frying pan and add the buns, cut side down into the butter. Leave to fry for a few minutes until lightly browed, then remove and fill with the lobster filling. Serve immediately or cover with cling film and chill before serving.

savoury eccles cakes

—Trendy twist on the classic

Eccles cakes are originally from the Lancashire town of Eccles. Traditionally they are served with Lancashire cheese but this modern twist on the classic is so fragrant and I almost prefer it. I have decided to try manchego cheese instead and it works wonderfully with the sherry in the filling to make a beautiful addition to your afternoon tea table.

makes
12

25g unsalted butter, in small cubes
30g good quality sherry
30g raw cane sugar
½ tsp ground allspice
½ orange, zest only
150g currants

250g plain flour + extra for dusting
150g water
250g block of butter

1 egg white
10g raw cane sugar
manchego cheese, to serve

prep:
2 hrs

1. To make the filling, place the butter, sherry, sugar, allspice and orange zest in the mixing bowl. Melt **3 Min. / 45°C / Speed 1**. Add the currants and combine **10 Sec. / Reverse / Speed 1**. Transfer to a small bowl and cover with cling film. Leave to infuse for 2 hours. Meanwhile, clean the mixing bowl.

2. To make the pastry, place the plain flour and water in the mixing bowl. Mix **20 Sec. / Speed 6**. Transfer to a bowl and cover with cling film. Refrigerate for 2 hours.

3. Put the block of butter between two sheets of greaseproof paper. Using a rolling pin, roll it into a 15cm x 15cm square, keeping the edges straight. Leave wrapped in the greaseproof paper and chill for 30 minutes. On a lightly floured surface, roll out the dough to a 30cm x 30cm square.

4. Place the butter on top at a 45° angle so that one edge of the butter is facing you. Fold over each corner of the dough to the centre to make a parcel. Use a pastry brush to brush off any flour. Press down the edges and flip upside down. Wrap in cling film and freeze for 10 minutes.

5. Once chilled, unwrap and roll out the dough to a rectangle of 20cm x 50cm. Roll out gently - do not press too hard, otherwise the butter will split. Fold the bottom third up, making sure that you keep brushing off the excess flour. Fold the top third down so that the dough is folded up like a letter. Wrap in cling film and freeze for 10 minutes. This is called a turn.

6. Remove from the freezer, unwrap and place the dough in front of you so that the folded edge faces your right. Repeat the same rolling out, folding, freezing process another three times. Preheat the oven to 200°C / 180°C Fan / Gas Mark 6. Line a large rectangular baking tray with greaseproof paper and set aside.

7. Unwrap the pastry and place on a floured surface. Roll out to a 2mm thick rectangle. Cut out equal numbers of circles with a 6.5cm and an 8.5cm cookie cutter. Place the smaller ones on the prepared tray, leaving some space in between each.

8. Uncover the soaked currants and drain any excess liquid. Place 1 tsp of the mixture on each small circle, leaving a border. Brush the border with some water and top with the larger circles, pressing them down to seal the filling. Chill for 20 minutes.

9. Remove from fridge and, using a 7cm cookie cutter, trim each eccles cake and cut 3 slits in the top. Brush with the egg white and sprinkle with the sugar. Bake in the oven for 20 minutes until golden brown. Transfer onto a wire cooling rack and leave to cool slightly before serving them with manchego cheese.

scones & buns

lemon curd

—Deliciously tangy

Lemon curd is a classic for afternoon tea. If you want to spice yours up a little, you can add some limoncello or passionfruit to the mixture. You could even replace the lemon with lime for a really lovely lime curd. Serve with scones and clotted cream.

makes
1 large
jar

240g golden caster sugar (or caster sugar)

2 lemons, zest

120g unsalted butter, in small cubes

3 large eggs

100g lemon juice (if you like it less tangy,
   use only 75g lemon juice)

prep:
25 min

1. Place the sugar in the mixing bowl. Blitz **10 Sec. / Speed 10**.
2. Add the lemon zest and blitz **20 Sec. / Speed 10**.
3. Add the butter, eggs and lemon juice and cook **20 Min. / 90°C / Speed 2 / no measuring cup**.
4. Once cooked, place the measuring cup on the lid and blend **25 Sec. / Speed 6**.
5. Pour into sterilised jars and leave to set. You can store the curd in the fridge for up to 4 weeks.

Tip: To make a limoncello curd, simply add 20g limoncello just before blending at the end.

apricot vanilla jam

—Heavenly

Apricot jam is my dad's favourite. I can't tell you how often he has mentioned to me to seal off cakes with boiling apricot jam to avoid getting crumbs into my buttercream icing. He always makes a big point about boiling the jam beforehand but sometimes I don't listen to that...not that I'd ever tell him. I hope you don't tell on me!

makes
1 large
jar

1000g apricots, pitted and halved
400g raw cane, jam or caster sugar
20g lemon juice
1 vanilla pod

prep:
30 min

1. Place the apricots in the mixing bowl. Blitz **2 Sec. / Speed 4**.
2. Add lemon juice, vanilla pod and 10g of the sugar and cook **15 Min. / Varoma / Reverse / Speed 4 / with simmering basket in place of measuring cup**. Should the mixture overboil, reduce the temperature down to 100°C and increase the cooking time by a further 4 minutes.
3. Add the remaining sugar and cook again **10 Min. / Varoma / Reverse / Speed 4 / with simmering basket in place of measuring cup**. Test whether the jam is set by placing a teaspoon of the jam on a cold plate; if it sets immediately and doesn't run off when tilting the plate, it is done. If not, cook for a further few minutes on the same setting as above. Remove the vanilla pod.
4. Pour the jam into sterilised jars and leave to set and cool. Store in a cool place for up to 4 weeks.

Tip: There are two ways to sterilise your jars. You can either place them in the sink and boil some water in a kettle. Once boiled, carefully pour the water over the jars and leave to cool slightly in the sink before rinsing. This can be dangerous so keep children away and exercise caution when pouring the boiling water into the sink. Alternatively, you can place the jars in the Varoma dish. Fill the mixing bowl with 1000g water and put the Varoma in place. Heat **15 Min. / Varoma / Speed 1**. Carefully remove the jars using oven gloves and leave to cool before filling.

apple & kiwi jam

—So refreshing

This jam is so gorgeous. It works perfectly with a freshly baked tea loaf or some classic scones. You can reduce the amount of sugar in the recipe and use agar agar instead if you wish.

makes
1 large
jar

600g kiwis, peeled and halved
400g apples, cored and quartered
350g raw cane, jam or caster sugar
1 lemon, juice only

prep:
25 min

1. Place the kiwis, apples, sugar and lemon juice in the mixing bowl. Blitz **5 Sec. / Speed 5**. Then cook **25 Min. / Varoma / Speed 1 / with simmering basket in place of measuring cup**. Test whether the jam is set by placing a teaspoon of the jam on a cold plate; if it sets immediately and doesn't run off when tilting the plate, it is done. If not, cook for a further few minutes on the same setting as above.
2. Pour the jam into sterilised jars and leave to set and cool. Store in a cool place for up to 4 weeks.

rhubarb & strawberry jam

—Serious taste explosion

I love all things rhubarb and strawberry and find it is such a classic jam for afternoon tea. Whether you use it as part of a recipe or to spread over your iced buns and scones, the combination of the two fruits is so gorgeous. You can also add some rose water to give it an oriental hint.

makes
1 large
jar

1 apple, cored and quartered
250g rhubarb, trimmed and cut into small
   pieces
250g strawberries
1 lemon, juice only
200g raw cane, jam or caster sugar
1 tsp vanilla bean paste (optional)

prep:
20 min

1. Place the apple, rhubarb, strawberries, lemon juice, sugar and vanilla in the mixing bowl. Chop **4 Sec. / Speed 5**. It should still be chunky. Cook **20 Min. / Varoma / Speed 1 / with simmering basket in place of measuring cup**. Test whether the jam is set by placing a teaspoon of the jam on a cold plate; if it sets immediately and doesn't run off when tilting the plate, it is done. If not, cook for a further few minutes on the same setting as above.
2. Pour the jam into sterilised jars and leave to set and cool. Store in a cool place for up to 4 weeks.

buttermilk scones

—With clotted cream and jam

Buttermilk scones are the classic afternoon tea treat. I don't think I have ever been to an afternoon tea ceremony without enjoying some of these delicious and fluffy cakes. There is debate about what you should be putting on first, the clotted cream or the jam but I would argue that it doesn't matter because once you eat them, nothing else will matter.

makes
10

225g plain flour + extra for dusting
1 Tbsp baking powder
1 pinch sea salt
25g unrefined golden caster sugar
50g unsalted butter, in small cubes
125g buttermilk
40g whole milk
1 large egg

1 tub clotted cream, to serve
1 jar raspberry jam, to serve

prep:
20 min

1. Preheat the oven to 200°C / 180°C Fan / Gas Mark 6. Line a large rectangular baking tray with greaseproof paper and set aside.
2. Place the plan flour, baking powder, sea salt, caster sugar, butter, buttermilk and whole milk in the mixing bowl. Combine **20 Sec. / Speed 6**. Don't worry if it is not fully incorporated, it is important not to over-beat scone dough.
3. Tip the dough onto a generously floured surface and very carefully, without overworking it, shape the dough into a 3cm thick disc. Cut out scones by dipping a fluted 5-6cm round cookie cutter into flour first and then pressing it down. Don't rotate the cookie cutter, otherwise you may lose the shape.
4. Place each scone on the baking tray with plenty of space (at least 4cm) in between. Brush each scone with egg and bake in the oven for 12-14 minutes until golden brown. Remove and leave to cool on a wire cooling rack. Serve with clotted cream and your favourite jam.

Tip: If you are using homemade buttermilk the consistency may be a little runnier so add up to an extra 150g plain flour and 1 tsp baking powder to achieve a better consistency.

blueberry scones

—Made with wholesome spelt

If you are looking for something that you can have for morning tea, these blueberry scones are the way to go. I love the flavour of spelt and it really adds some great texture to these scones. They are slightly different and will not rise as much as the traditional buttermilk scone but they are so delicious.

makes
8-10

350g spelt flour + extra for dusting
4 tsp baking powder
1 pinch sea salt
125g unsalted butter, in small cubes
75g light soft brown sugar
175g buttermilk

20g whole milk
150g fresh or frozen blueberries (thawed
    if frozen)
1 large egg

blueberry jam, to serve

1. Preheat the oven to 200°C / 180°C Fan / Gas Mark 6. Line two large rectangular baking trays with greaseproof paper and set aside.
2. Place the spelt flour, baking powder, sea salt, butter, sugar, buttermilk and whole milk in the mixing bowl. Combine **20 Sec. / Speed 6**. Don't worry if it is not fully incorporated, it is important not to over-beat scone dough.
3. Tip the dough onto a generously floured surface. Add the blueberries to the dough and carefully, without overworking the dough, work in the blueberries and shape it into a 3cm-thick round disc.
4. Cut out scones by dipping a fluted 5-6cm round cookie cutter into flour first and then pressing it down. Don't rotate the cookie cutter, otherwise you may lose the shape. Alternatively, for triangular scones, cut the round disc into 8 even pieces like a cake.
5. Place the scones on prepared baking tray with plenty of space (at least 4cm) in between. Brush each scone with egg and bake in the oven for 12-14 minutes until golden brown. Remove and leave to cool on a wire cooling rack. Serve with fresh blueberry jam.

Tip: Instead of blueberries you can also use raspberries. If you are using frozen fruit, just make sure they are thawed before using.

raspberry scones

—With cacao nibs

Who says you cannot have a fluffy scone when you are gluten intolerant? I think we might have to prove them wrong with these majesties of scones, filled with delicious freeze-dried raspberries (one of my favourite inventions ever) and cacao nibs. They are not too sweet and taste super delicious served with some homemade chocolate hazelnut spread.

makes
12

375g gluten free plain flour + extra for
    dusting
1 Tbsp gluten free baking powder
1 pinch sea salt
80g icing sugar
2 tsp xanthan gum
30g unsalted butter, in small cubes

1 large egg
330g buttermilk
20g freeze-dried raspberries
    (or strawberries)
20g cacao nibs

chocolate hazelnut spread, to serve

prep:
20 min

1. Preheat the oven to 200°C / 180°C Fan / Gas Mark 6. Line two large rectangular baking trays with greaseproof paper and set aside.
2. Place the gluten free plain flour, gluten free baking powder, sea salt, icing sugar, xanthan gum, butter, egg, buttermilk, raspberries and cacao nibs in the mixing bowl. Combine **20 Sec. / Speed 6**. Don't worry if it is not fully incorporated, it is important not to over-beat scone dough.
3. Tip the dough onto a generously floured surface and very carefully, without overworking it, shape the dough into a 3cm thick disc.
4. Cut out scones by dipping a fluted 5-6cm round cookie cutter into flour first and then pressing it down. Don't rotate the cookie cutter, otherwise you may lose the shape. Place each scone on the tray with plenty of space (at least 4cm) in between. Brush each scone with egg and bake in the oven for 12-14 minutes until golden brown. Remove and leave to cool on a wire cooling rack. Serve with some homemade chocolate hazelnut spread.

Tip: Most larger supermarkets sell gluten free plain flour. I use Dove's Farm because it is superb quality. If you cannot find it in your local supermarket, try online – I usually order the flour in bulk directly from Dove's Farm.

gingerbread scones

—Enjoy with gingered butter

On a cold and rainy day there is nothing better than the taste of warm spices to make you feel cozy and nice. These gingerbread scones contain all of that and more. Made with wholemeal flour and fragrant ginger, they are ideal if you are looking for something a little more individual. They are best served with some gingered butter and your favourite marmalade (I like orange marmalade).

makes
10

125g plain flour + extra for dusting
100g wholemeal flour
1 Tbsp baking powder
1 pinch sea salt
25g golden caster sugar
50g unsalted butter, in small cubes
125g buttermilk

40g whole milk
1 tsp ground ginger
½ tsp ground cinnamon
1 large egg

30g stem ginger
100g unsalted butter, in small cubes

prep:
20 min

1. Preheat the oven to 200°C / 180°C Fan / Gas Mark 6. Line a large rectangular baking tray with greaseproof paper and set aside.

2. Place the plain flour, wholemeal flour, baking powder, sea salt, caster sugar, butter, buttermilk, whole milk, ground ginger and ground cinnamon in the mixing bowl. Combine **20 Sec. / Speed 6**. Don't worry if it is not fully incorporated, it is important not to over-beat scone dough.

3. Tip the dough onto a generously floured surface and very carefully, without overworking it, shape the dough into a 3cm thick disc. Cut out scones by dipping a fluted 5-6cm round cookie cutter into flour first and then pressing it down. Don't rotate the cookie cutter, otherwise you may lose the shape. Place each scone on the tray with plenty of space (at least 4cm) in between. Brush each scone with egg and bake in the oven for 12-14 minutes until golden brown. Remove and leave to cool on a wire cooling rack.

4. To make the ginger butter, place the stem ginger in the mixing bowl. Blitz **2 Sec. / Speed 7**. Scrape down using spatula. Then add the butter and combine **30 Sec. / Speed 5**. Serve the scones with the gingered butter and your favourite jam.

cheesy scones

—With feta, chives and rosemary

On a hunt for something savoury? These cheesy scones are just perfect for those of us who like it on the savoury side of life. They are flavoured with fragrant rosemary and tasty chives and feta cheese. It is like an explosion of delicious ingredients.

makes
10

3 sprigs rosemary, stalks removed
25g chives, finely chopped
50g feta cheese
225g plain flour + extra for dusting
1 Tbsp baking powder

1 pinch sea salt
50g unsalted butter, in small cubes
125g buttermilk
1 pinch sea salt
1 pinch black pepper

prep:
20 min

1. Preheat the oven to 200°C / 180°C Fan / Gas Mark 6. Line a large rectangular baking tray with greaseproof paper and set aside.
2. Place the rosemary in the mixing bowl. Blitz **3 Sec. / Speed 7**. Add the chives, feta cheese, plain flour, baking powder, sea salt, butter, buttermilk, sea salt and black pepper and combine **20 Sec. / Speed 6**. Don't worry if it is not fully incorporated, it is important not to over-beat scone dough.
3. Tip the dough onto a generously floured surface and very carefully, without overworking it, shape the dough into a 3cm thick disc.
4. Cut out scones by dipping a fluted 5-6cm round cookie cutter into flour first and then pressing it down. Don't rotate the cookie cutter, otherwise you may lose the shape. Place each scone on the tray with plenty of space (at least 4cm) in between. Bake in the oven for 12-14 minutes until golden brown. Remove and leave to cool on a wire cooling rack. Serve with some cream cheese and chive schmear (p. 31).

pumpkin scones

—Super colourful

Pumpkin scones are so vibrant and colourful. I love them savoury and sweet. This version is a mixture and contains some grated Parmesan cheese to add some nutty flavour. You can serve it with some fresh butter and a chutney of your choice. I think mango chutney would go quite well.

makes
10

30g Parmesan cheese, in small chunks
100g cooked, puréed pumpkin
30g unsalted butter, in small cubes
40g caster sugar
1 egg

375g plain flour + extra for dusting
1 pinch black pepper
1 pinch sea salt
80g buttermilk

prep:
20 min

1. Preheat the oven to 200°C / 180°C Fan / Gas Mark 6. Line a large rectangular baking tray with greaseproof paper and set aside.
2. Place the Parmesan in the mixing bowl and chop **5 Sec. / Speed 7**. Add the pumpkin, butter, caster sugar, egg, plain flour, black pepper, salt and buttermilk and combine **20 Sec. / Speed 6**. Depending on the consistency of the pumpkin, the mixture may be too thick or too thin – add more buttermilk or flour depending on its consistency. Don't worry if it is not fully incorporated, it is important not to over-beat scone dough.
3. Tip the dough onto a generously floured surface and very carefully, without overworking it, shape the dough into a 3cm thick disc.
4. Cut out scones by dipping a fluted 5-6cm round cookie cutter into flour first and then pressing it down. Don't rotate the cookie cutter, otherwise you may lose the shape. Place each scone on the tray with plenty of space (at least 4cm) in between. Brush each scone with egg and bake in the oven for 12-14 minutes until golden brown. Remove and leave to cool on a wire cooling rack. Serve cold with some fresh butter.

Tip: To cook your pumpkin, simply chop into small dice and place in the simmering basket. Fill the mixing bowl with 1000g water and insert the simmering basket. Cook **30 Min. / 100°C / Speed 1**. Drain the water and place the cooked pumpkin in the mixing bowl. Purée **10. Sec. / Speed 8**. Leave to cool before using.

raspberry iced buns

—A British classic

Do you want something for afternoon tea that is really easy to make? These raspberry iced buns would definitely be on my list. Actually, you don't even have to use freeze-dried raspberries. You can also top with some sugar sprinkles or chocolate sprinkles over the icing and even get the kids involved to prepare them.

makes
20

220g whole milk
1 Tbsp dry active yeast (or 30g fresh yeast)
50g golden caster sugar (or caster sugar)
80g unsalted butter, in small cubes
500g strong white bread flour + extra for
  dusting
1 large egg
1 tsp sea salt

350g icing sugar
a few drops pink food colouring
  (or gel colouring)
10g freeze-dried raspberries

prep:
2-3 hrs

1. Line two large rectangular baking trays with greaseproof paper and set aside.
2. Place the whole milk, yeast and caster sugar in the mixing bowl. Warm **2 Min. / 37°C / Speed 2.5**. Add the butter, flour, egg and salt and knead **2 Min. / Kneading Function**. Tip the dough into a bowl and cover with cling film. Leave to rise for 1-2 hours at room temperature until doubled in size.
3. Uncover the dough and tip onto a lightly floured surface and divide into 20 pieces. Shape each piece into a sausage shape and place onto the prepared baking tray. You can sit them quite closely to get soft edges or well apart to get perfect round buns. Cover with a tea towel and leave to rise for another 30 minutes. Meanwhile preheat the oven to 200°C / 180°C Fan / Gas Mark 6.
4. Bake the buns in the oven for 10-12 minutes until lightly golden. Transfer onto a wire cooling rack and leave to cool.
5. To make the icing, place the icing sugar in a large bowl. Add enough water to make a thick, cream-like mixture. Dip each cooled bun in the icing then sprinkle with raspberries. You can also add some food colouring to the icing and make them pink.

Tip: You can prepare these buns a day ahead and store them in a bread bag for up to three days. Ice just before serving.

earl grey teacakes

—Perfect with some butter

These lovely, fruity rolls are just perfect for teatime. Enjoy them with your favourite marmalade and you have yourself a classic afternoon tea treat. You can make six large or twelve small rolls with this recipe.

makes
12

200g water
2 Earl Grey teabags
200g mixed dried fruit

250g whole milk
1 Tbsp dry active yeast (or 30g fresh yeast)
50g caster sugar

80g unsalted butter, in small cubes
500g strong white bread flour + extra for
    dusting
1 large egg
1 tsp sea salt

50g apricot jam (p. 41)

prep:
2-3 hrs

soak:
overnight

1. The evening before you want to make the buns, boil the kettle and pour the water in a jug. Add the Earl Grey teabags and leave to infuse for 10 minutes. Remove the teabags and add the dried fruit. Cover and leave to soak overnight in the fridge.
2. The next day, line two large rectangular baking trays with greaseproof paper and set aside. Remove the fruit from the fridge and discard any leftover liquid.
3. Place the whole milk, yeast and caster sugar in the mixing bowl. Warm **2 Min. / 37°C / Speed 2.5**. Add the butter, flour, egg, soaked fruit and salt and knead **2 Min. / Kneading Function**. Tip the dough into a bowl and cover with cling film. Leave to rise for 1-2 hours at room temperature until doubled in size.
4. Uncover the dough and tip onto a lightly floured surface. Divide into 12 equal pieces and roll each into a ball. Place on the prepared trays and cover with a tea towel. Leave to rest for another 30 minutes. Preheat the oven to 200°C / 180°C Fan / Gas Mark 6.
5. Bake the buns in the oven for 15 minutes. Meanwhile, heat the apricot jam in a small saucepan.
6. Remove the buns from the oven and brush them with the apricot jam. Transfer onto a wire cooling rack. Leave to cool.
7. Serve with butter and your favourite jam or marmalade.

mini cinnamon scrolls

—With a lemony icing

Oh heavenly cinnamon rolls! I must admit, I am quite obsessed with them. And, although not a traditional afternoon tea serving, I think they make a wonderful addition to an afternoon tea table. Especially because of their size, you can nibble away at them and still be able to enjoy lots of other goodies.

makes
24

220g whole milk
1 Tbsp dry active yeast (or 30g fresh yeast)
50g caster sugar
80g unsalted butter, in small cubes
350g strong white bread flour + extra for
  dusting
150g wholemeal bread flour
1 large egg
1 tsp sea salt

80g butter
80g brown sugar
2 tsp ground cinnamon

1 lemon, juice only
400g icing sugar

prep:
2-3 hrs

1. Line two large rectangular baking trays with greaseproof paper and set aside.
2. Place the whole milk, yeast and caster sugar in the mixing bowl. Warm **2 Min. / 37°C / Speed 2.5**. Add the butter, strong white bread flour, wholemeal bread flour, egg and salt and knead **2 Min. / Kneading Function**. Tip the dough into a bowl and cover with cling film. Leave to rise for 1-2 hours at room temperature until doubled in size. Clean the mixing bowl.
3. Uncover the dough and tip onto a lightly floured surface. Roll out to a large rectangle approx. 70cm x 20cm.
4. Place butter in mixing bowl and melt **3 Min. / 55°C / Speed 1**. Brush over the rectangle, followed by the sugar and cinnamon. Roll up away from you using one long end. Make a tight roll and cut into 24 mini cinnamon rolls. Place them on the prepared trays well apart. Cover with a tea towel and leave to rise for another 30 minutes. Meanwhile preheat the oven to 200°C / 180°C Fan / Gas Mark 6.
5. Bake the cinnamon buns in the oven for 10-12 minutes until golden brown. Remove and place on a wire cooling rack. Leave to cool. Clean the mixing bowl.
6. Place the icing sugar and lemon juice in the mixing bowl. Combine **20 Sec. / Speed 3**. It should be like thick cream. Drizzle over the cooled cinnamon buns and leave to harden before serving.

cakes

- Vegan Sponge
- Gluten Free Sponge
- Raspberry Crème Genoise
- Mini Black Forest Gateaux
- Lavender Honey Cake
- Omi's Cherry Cake
- Orange & Almond Victoria Sponge
- Battenberg
- Apple Spiced Tea Loaf
- Hazelnut & Apricot Roulade
- Fragrant Rose Cake
- Coffee & Walnut Cake
- Macadamia Brownies
- Apple & Pecan Cake
- Rhubarb Cheesecake

vegan sponge

—Vanilla and chocolate

makes
2 sponges

300g dairy free margarine (suitable
  for baking)
300g gluten free plain flour
300g raw cane sugar
1 tsp vanilla extract
200g soya yoghurt

prep:
50 min

1 tsp xanthan gum
1½ Tbsp baking powder
75g oat milk (or rice or almond)

For chocolate sponge
50g cocoa powder
50g oat milk

1. Preheat the oven to 180°C / 160°C Fan / Gas Mark 4. Line two 18cm round springform cake tins with greaseproof paper and set aside.
2. Place the margarine, gluten free plain flour, sugar, vanilla extract, soya yoghurt, xanthan gum, baking powder and oat milk in the mixing bowl. Combine **20 Sec. / Speed 5**. Scrape down using spatula, then mix again **20 Sec. / Speed 5** (if you are making the chocolate version, add the cocoa powder and milk to the bowl as well).
3. Divide the mixture between the two tins and bake in the oven for 30-35 minutes until golden brown and a skewer inserted comes out clean. Leave to cool in the tin for 5 minutes, then tip upside down onto a wire cooling rack and leave to cool. Now you can use the sponges as desired to fill, cut and decorate.

gluten free sponge

—Vanilla and chocolate

makes
2 sponges

225g unsalted butter, in small cubes
4 large eggs
225g gluten free plain flour
225g raw cane sugar
1 Tbsp baking powder
1 tsp xanthan gum

prep:
50 min

1 tsp vanilla extract
75g whole milk

For chocolate sponge
50g cocoa powder
50g whole milk

1. Preheat the oven to 180°C / 160°C Fan / Gas Mark 4. Line two 18cm round springform cake tins with greaseproof paper and set aside.
2. Place the butter in the mixing bowl. Blitz **40 Sec. / Speed 5**. Scrape down using spatula.
3. Add the eggs, gluten free plain flour, sugar, baking powder, xanthan gum and vanilla extract and combine **30 Sec. / Speed 5**. If you are making the chocolate version, add the cocoa powder and milk to the bowl as well.
4. Divide the mixture between the two tins and bake in the oven for 30-35 minutes until golden brown and a skewer inserted comes out clean. Leave to cool in the tin for 5 minutes, then tip upside down onto a wire cooling rack and leave to cool. Now you can use the sponges as desired to fill, cut and decorate.

raspberry crème genoise

—Fluffy crème pâtissière

In the summer there is nothing better than having fresh fruit and a light cake. A genoise is exactly what you need when you are throwing a summer afternoon tea party. Genoise is a very light sponge made without butter. It is a perfect partner for the fluffy crème pâtissière that is used in this recipe, and the raspberries make it a superb treat that you can even serve frozen.

serves
10

4 large eggs
120g golden caster sugar (or caster sugar)
1 tsp vanilla extract
80g plain flour
40g ground almonds
1 tsp baking powder
1 pinch salt

500g whole milk

1 vanilla pod, scraped
4 egg yolks
100g golden caster sugar (or caster sugar)
40g unsalted butter, in small cubes
50g cornflour
1 tsp vanilla extract
250g double cream (or thickened cream)
300g fresh raspberries (or frozen, thawed)
icing sugar to dust

prep:
1 hr

chill:
1 hr

1. Preheat the oven to 180°C / 160°C Fan / Gas Mark 4. Line a 20cm x 30cm rectangular baking tin with greaseproof paper and set aside.
2. Insert the butterfly whisk. Place the eggs, caster sugar and vanilla extract in the mixing bowl. Whisk **6 Min. / 37°C / Speed 4**. Whisk again **6 Min. / Speed 4 / no measuring cup** (no temperature).
3. Add the plain flour, ground almonds, baking powder and salt to either side of the butterfly whisk in the mixing bowl. Combine **4 Sec. / Speed 3**. Remove the butterfly whisk. At this stage you need to very carefully tip the mixture onto the prepared tray and spread out evenly to make a large rectangle. Bake in the oven for 10-15 minutes until lightly golden and fluffy.
4. Remove sponge from the oven and turn upside down onto a wire cooling rack. Remove the greaseproof paper and leave to cool. Meanwhile, clean the mixing bowl.
5. To make the crème pâtissière, place the milk, scraped vanilla and pod, egg yolks, sugar, butter, cornflour and vanilla extract in the cleaned mixing bowl. Cook **9 Min. / 90°C / Speed 3**. Remove the vanilla pod, transfer to a large bowl and cover the top with cling film to avoid a skin from forming. Leave to set and cool for at least 1 hour. Clean the mixing bowl.
6. Insert the butterfly whisk. Pour in the double cream. Whisk on **Speed 4** until stiff, watching carefully to avoid over-whipping (this could take anywhere from 20-45 seconds). Transfer to a large bowl.
7. Add the cooled crème pâtissière to the bowl and combine with a whisk until fluffy. Add the raspberries and fold in very gently.
8. Cut the cooled genoise into two squares that fit into a 20cm square tin. Line the square tin with cling film and place the first square of genoise in the bottom. Spread the raspberry crème pâtissière over it, then top with the other square. Press down slightly and chill for at least 2 hours or freeze for 1 hour until set.
9. Carefully lift out the cake using the cling film as a lifting tool. Remove the cling film and, using a hot and wet knife, cut the cake into slices and dust with icing sugar. Serve chilled or even frozen on a hot summer's day.

black forest mini gâteaux

—A German tradition

Black Forest Gâteau owes its name to the area of Germany where it originated. The gâteau is distinctive because of the cherry liqueur Kirsch, which is the schnapps used to give this cake its unique flavour. I love these mini versions which are a little messy and so perfect for afternoon tea because they are bite-sized and look gorgeous next to other colourful treats.

serves
8

340g butter
340g caster sugar
2 tsp vanilla extract
6 large eggs
340g plain flour
2 Tbsp baking powder
50g cocoa powder
4 Tbsp hot water
2 Tbsp dark rum (or more water)

250g cherry juice (or liquid from the cherry jar)
25g cornflour
30g caster sugar
1 Tbsp Kirsch (optional)
500g pitted sour cherries (fresh from a glass jar or frozen, defrosted)
600g double cream (or thickened cream)

prep:
3 hrs

1. Preheat the oven to 180°C / 160°C Fan / Gas Mark 4. Line a large rectangular tray with greaseproof paper and set aside.
2. Place butter, caster sugar, vanilla extract, eggs, plain flour and baking powder in the mixing bowl. Mix **30 Sec. / Speed 5**. Scrape down using spatula.
3. Place the cocoa powder in a bowl and pour over the boiling water and rum. Add to the batter and mix **20 Sec. / Speed 5**.
4. Pour the batter into the prepared baking tray and bake in the oven for 25-25 minutes until a skewer inserted comes out clean. Remove and transfer onto a wire cooling rack. Leave to cool. Meanwhile, clean the mixing bowl.
5. Pour the cherry juice, cornflour, caster sugar and Kirsch (optional) in the mixing bowl. Cook **5 Min. / 90°C / Speed 2**. Add the cherries and combine **20 Sec. / Reverse / Speed 2**. Pour into a small bowl and leave to cool. Clean the mixing bowl again.
6. Insert the butterfly whisk. Add the cream and whisk on Speed 4 until stiff, watching carefully to avoid over-whipping (this could take anywhere from 20-45 seconds).
7. To assemble the cakes, take the cooled sponge and cut out mini circles approx. 5cm diameter. Place some cherries on one of the sponges, spoon over some cream and top with another sponge piece. Finish off with some more cherries. Repeat until everything is used up. Chill before serving.

lavender honey cake

—With a zingy twist

Jesse loves lavender and recently I have been experimenting with spelt flour which is how this beautiful creation came about, and it is such a tasty and flavoursome cake for afternoon tea. The lavender honey adds a special twist and the cake goes super well with Earl Grey tea. Perfect for a summery afternoon tea.

makes
16 slices

150g unsalted butter, in small cubes + extra
    for greasing
180g raw cane sugar
1 tsp vanilla extract
50g lavender honey (or normal honey + 1 tsp
    dried lavender)
3 large eggs
280g Greek style yoghurt

300g white spelt flour + extra for greasing
1 Tbsp baking powder
½ tsp ground cinnamon

60g lemon juice
60g lavender honey (or normal honey)
250g unrefined golden icing sugar
2 tsp dried lavender

prep:
1 hr

chill:
1 hr

1. Preheat the oven to 180°C / 160°C Fan / Gas Mark 4. Grease a Bundt cake tin with butter and dust with flour.
2. Place the butter in the mixing bowl. Blitz **40 sec. / Speed 5**. Scrape down using spatula.
3. Add the caster sugar, vanilla extract, lavender honey, eggs, Greek style yoghurt, spelt flour, baking powder and cinnamon and combine **30 Sec. / Speed 5**.
4. Pour the mixture into the prepared cake tin and bake for 35-45 minutes until golden brown and a skewer inserted comes out clean. Remove from oven and leave to cool in the tin for 5 minutes, then tip upside down onto a wire cooling rack and leave to cool completely. Clean the mixing bowl.
5. To make the icing, place the lemon juice, lavender honey and icing sugar in the mixing bowl. Combine **20 Sec. / Speed 3**. Pour over the cooled cake and let it run down the sides. Sprinkle with the dried lavender and leave to harden before serving.

Tip: If you cannot find lavender honey, you can make your own by heating 200g high quality runny honey with 2 Tbsp dried lavender until boiling. Then fill into sterilised jars and leave to infuse for one week before using.

omi's cherry cake

—Very traditional

The taste of fresh cherries reminds me of early summertime in Germany. Our region is known for its cherries. They are so beautifully rich and juicy, and my grandma makes a great cherry jelly. She is also known for her beautiful cherry cake, which is a soft and light sponge made with yoghurt and oil instead of butter. A delicious treat for afternoon tea and the flaked almonds add a lovely crust.

serves
6-8

125g golden caster sugar (or caster sugar)
3 large eggs
125g Greek style yoghurt
1 tsp vanilla extract
1 Tbsp baking powder
250g plain flour
65g rapeseed oil
400g pitted sour cherries (fresh or frozen,
   defrosted)
icing sugar to dust

prep:
1 hr

1. Preheat the oven to 180°C / 160°C Fan / Gas Mark 4. Line a 20cm square tin with greaseproof paper.
2. Drain the cherries and pat dry with a kitchen towel.
3. Place the golden caster sugar, eggs, Greek style yoghurt, vanilla extract, baking powder, plain flour and rapeseed oil in the mixing bowl. Combine **30 Sec. / Speed 5**.
4. Pour the mixture into the prepared tin. Dot the cherries evenly on top, being careful not to press them too far into the batter. Bake for 35-40 minutes until a skewer inserted comes out clean. Remove from the oven and transfer onto a wire cooling rack. Leave to cool, then dust with icing sugar and cut into slices.

Tip: Usually you can buy sour cherries in a jar. They are available from larger supermarkets in the international aisle. If not, use frozen cherries but make sure they are fully defrosted before use.

orange & almond victoria sponge

—So fluffy and fragrant

This summery orange and almond sponge is the perfect cake for a light afternoon tea party. The orange flavoured sponge is so fluffy and goes super well with orange marmalade. I find the look of a savarin cake tin really adds a nice touch for the eye as well.

makes
16 slices

185g unsalted butter, in small cubes + extra
  for greasing
1 tsp vanilla extract
1 tsp orange extract
165g unrefined caster sugar
3 large eggs
60g whole milk
225g plain flour + extra for dusting
1 Tbsp baking powder

40g flaked almonds
300g heavy whipping cream
40g unrefined icing sugar
½ tsp orange extract
300g orange marmalade, thin cut

prep:
2 hrs

1. Preheat the oven to 180°C / 160°C Fan / Gas Mark 4. Grease a 20cm savarin mould with butter and dust with plain flour.
2. Place the unsalted butter, vanilla extract, orange extract, unrefined caster sugar, eggs, whole milk, plain flour and baking powder in the mixing bowl. Combine **40 Sec. / Speed 5**. Pour into the prepared tin and bake for 30-35 minutes until golden brown and a skewer inserted comes out clean. Remove the sponge and turn it upside down onto a wire cooling rack. Leave to cool completely.
3. While the oven is still hot, toast the almond flakes on a baking tray for 3-4 minutes. Leave to cool. Clean mixing bowl.
4. Insert butterfly whisk and add the whipping cream, icing sugar and orange extract. Whisk on Speed 4 until stiff, watching carefully to avoid over-whipping (this could take anywhere from 20-45 seconds).
5. Warm the orange marmalade in a small saucepan until hot.
6. Cut the cooled cake into three even layers. Spread one third of the marmalade over it, then place another layer of sponge on top. Repeat the orange and sponge layering until it is used up. Spread two thirds of the cream around the sides of the cake and decorate with the flaked almonds. Spoon the remaining cream into a piping bag fitted with a star nozzle. Pipe little rosettes on top of the cake and dust with icing sugar.

battenberg

—Chocolate & vanilla beauty

Battenberg is like having the royals over for tea. It is a classic and this chocolate and vanilla version looks genius as well. If you are on a mission to impress the guests, this is definitely one to try. It takes a little while to get how it works but it is worth it and you can easily make a raspberry and vanilla version by using raspberry jam instead and a little drop of pink food colouring instead of cocoa powder for the sponge.

serves
6

280g unsalted butter, in small cubes
5 large eggs
280g plain flour
2 tsp vanilla extract
1½ Tbsp baking powder
280g golden caster sugar (or caster sugar)
30g cocoa powder
40g whole milk

100g chocolate hazelnut spread
 (or Notella), softened
500g ready to roll marzipan
10g icing sugar
60g apricot jam (p. 41)
10g cocoa powder

prep:
2 hrs

1. Preheat the oven to 180°C / 160°C Fan / Gas Mark 4. Line a 20cm square tin with greaseproof paper and set aside.
2. Place the butter in the mixing bowl. Blitz **40 Sec. / Speed 5**. Scrape down using spatula.
3. Add the eggs, plain flour, vanilla extract, baking powder and caster sugar and combine **20 Sec. / Speed 5**. Scrape down and combine again **10 Sec. / Speed 5**.
4. Pour half the mixture (approx. 550g) into the prepared tin and bake 20-25 minutes until a skewer inserted comes out clean.
5. Meanwhile, add the cocoa powder and milk to the other half of the batter and combine **10 Sec. / Speed 5**. Once the first sponge is baked, remove from the oven and tip onto wire cooling rack. Line the square tin with greaseproof paper again and pour chocolate batter into it. Bake for 20-25 minutes until a skewer inserted comes out clean. Tip it onto a wire cooling rack and leave to cool.
6. Once the cakes are cool, place one sponge on top of the other one and straighten the edges and level the surface with a knife. Spread the top of the vanilla sponge with hazelnut spread and lay the chocolate sponge on top. Gently press them together. Cut into 4 long, even strips.
7. Flip one strip over onto its side and spread with chocolate hazelnut spread. Then take a second strip, rotate it 180 degrees and lay it on top of the first strip to form a chequerboard cake. Repeat with the remaining strips. You should end up with two Battenberg logs.
8. To finish it off, cut the marzipan in half and slightly dust the work surface with icing sugar. Roll out one piece of marzipan to a square which is as long as one Battenberg log. Warm the apricot jam in a small saucepan over medium heat until bubbling. Brush over the marzipan lightly and lay one Battenberg log onto the edge of the marzipan nearest you. Trim the edge of the marzipan to fit, then roll over the cake into the marzipan so that all sides of it are covered in marzipan. Trim off any excess and set aside.
9. Add the cocoa powder to the other piece of marzipan and knead until combined. Dust the work surface in cocoa powder and repeat as above with the other Battenberg log. You should end up with one black and one white Battenberg which you can cut up and serve on a large serving plate.

apple spiced tea loaf

—With mixed dried fruit

There can be no traditional afternoon tea without a fruity tea loaf. This special apple and mixed spice tea loaf is packed with beautiful spices that will fill your afternoon tea table with lovely aromas. You can store it in a cake tin for up to one week.

makes
16 slices

1 apple, halved
½ lemon, juice only
175g unsalted butter, in small cubes
175g light soft brown sugar
3 large eggs
1 tsp vanilla extract
85g ground almonds

1 Tbsp baking powder
175g plain flour
1 tsp ground cinnamon
½ tsp ground nutmeg
200g dried mixed fruit
1 Tbsp apricot jam (p. 41)

prep:
2 hrs

1. Preheat the oven to 180°C / 160°C Fan / Gas Mark 4. Line a 1-pound loaf tin with greaseproof paper and set aside.
2. Slice one apple half into thin slices and drizzle with lemon juice. Set aside until later.
3. Place other half of the apple in the mixing bowl. Blitz **5 Sec. / Speed 5**. Scrape down using spatula. Add the butter, sugar, eggs, vanilla extract, ground almonds, baking powder, plain flour, ground cinnamon and ground nutmeg and combine **30 Sec. / Speed 5**. Add the mixed dried fruit and combine again **10 Sec. / Reverse / Speed 3**. Finish combining dried fruit into mixture with spatula if necessary. Transfer batter to prepared tin and decorate with the sliced apple.
4. Bake in the oven for 45 minutes, then turn down the oven to 140°C / 120°C Fan / Gas Mark 1 and cover the cake with foil. Bake for a further 45 minutes until a skewer inserted comes out clean. Remove and leave to cool for 10 minutes in the tin, then lift onto a wire cooling rack and leave to cool.
5. Heat the apricot jam in a small saucepan until bubbling. Brush over the top of the cake and leave to set before slicing.

Tip: Spread some jam over the tea loaf and serve it like a slice of fruit bread.

hazelnut & apricot roulade

—A delicious summer treat

This nutty sponge roll tastes absolutely delicious. In this recipe you can learn how to make your own hazelnut praline, which tastes so gorgeous paired with the zingy taste of apricot jam. Definitely a showstopper for the afternoon tea table.

**makes
8 slices**

80g plain flour
40g whole hazelnuts
½ lemon, zest only
4 eggs
120g golden caster sugar (or caster sugar)
1 tsp vanilla extract
1 tsp baking powder

100g whole hazelnuts
100g golden caster sugar
10g water

500g heavy whipping cream
250g apricot jam
icing sugar to dust

**prep:
3 hrs**

1. Preheat the oven to 180°C / 160°C Fan / Gas Mark 4. Line a large rectangular baking tray (at least 25cm x 35cm if not larger) with greaseproof paper and set aside.
2. Place the plain flour, whole hazelnuts and lemon zest in the mixing bowl. Blitz **10 Sec. / Speed 10**. Transfer into a small bowl and set aside. Rinse the mixing bowl.
3. Insert the butterfly whisk. Place the eggs, caster sugar and vanilla extract in the mixing bowl. Whisk **6 Min. / 37°C / Speed 4**. Whisk again **6 Min. / Speed 4 / no measuring cup** (no temperature).
4. Carefully add the reserved flour mixture to either side of the whisk attachment with the baking powder and combine **4 Sec. / Speed 3**. Remove the butterfly whisk.
5. Carefully tip the mixture onto the prepared tray and spread out evenly to make a large rectangle. Bake in the oven for 10-15 minutes until lightly golden and fluffy. Meanwhile, prepare another large sheet of greaseproof paper. Once the cake is baked, tip it out onto the prepared sheet and remove the greaseproof paper attached to the sponge from the oven. Carefully roll up the Swiss roll immediately, beginning on one short end. Then wrap in a clean tea towel and place aside. It should be enclosed in the towel and rolled up nicely (it does not have to be rolled tightly). Clean the mixing bowl.
6. While the oven is still hot, place the hazelnuts onto a small baking tray. Roast for 3-4 minutes, then tip into the mixing bowl and chop **2 Sec. / Speed 4**. Set aside.
7. Place the sugar and water in a small saucepan and dissolve over low heat without stirring. Bring to the boil and cook until the syrup turns a caramel/amber colour. Stir in the hazelnuts and coat for 30 seconds. Tip the hazelnuts onto a baking tray lined with greaseproof paper and leave until hardened and cooled. Break up into chunks and place in the mixing bowl. Blitz **2 Sec. / Speed 4**. Transfer the hazelnut praline into a small bowl. Clean mixing bowl.
8. Insert the butterfly whisk. Place whipping cream in mixing bowl and whisk on Speed 4 until stiff, watching carefully to avoid over-whipping (this could take anywhere from 20-45 seconds). Add half the hazelnut praline and incorporate with your spatula.
9. Once the roll is cooled (feel the towel – if it is still warm, leave it for a bit longer) remove the towel and unroll the Swiss roll. Spread evenly with the jam, then top with half the hazelnut praline cream. Roll it up again and place it seam-side down onto a fresh piece of greaseproof paper. Chill for 20 minutes. Then spread the remaining hazelnut praline cream over the roll and scatter the remaining hazelnut praline onto a piece of greaseproof paper. Roll the coated Swiss roll in the praline and dust with icing sugar. Chill before serving.

fragrant rose cake

—Three Layers Of Perfection

English roses are the most beautiful flowers in the world. My mum and I have always loved roses and I actually made this rose cake one Mother's Day for her. It is such a stunning afternoon tea cake and you can prepare it a day in advance – simply chill until serving. This recipe makes a very big cake and is large enough for a crowd.

serves
10

350g unsalted butter, in small cubes
500g golden caster sugar (or caster sugar)
6 large eggs
200g Greek style yoghurt
500g plain flour
2 Tbsp baking powder
2 tsp vanilla extract
2 tsp rose water

140g golden caster sugar
1 tsp rosewater
85g fresh raspberries (or frozen, thawed)
250g icing sugar
300g double cream (or thickened cream)

150g raspberries
rose petals

prep:
3 hrs

1. Preheat the oven to 180°C / 160°C Fan / Gas Mark 4. Line three 20cm round springform cake tins with greaseproof paper. If you don't have three tins, you can bake the cakes one by one.
2. Place 175g butter in the mixing bowl. Blitz **40 Sec. / Speed 5**. Scrape down using spatula. Add 250g caster sugar, 3 eggs, 100g yoghurt, 250g plain flour, 1 Tbsp baking powder, 1 tsp vanilla extract and 1 tsp rose water. Combine **40 Sec. / Speed 5** while inserting your spatula through hole in mixing bowl lid and helping the batter to be fully incorporated. Transfer to a large bowl. Repeat with the other half of the ingredients. Divide the batter between the three cake tins or start with a third of the batter and cover the remaining batter with cling film if you are only using one tin. Bake for 35-45 minutes until a skewer inserted comes out clean. Place each cake onto a wire cooling rack, remove from the tin and tip upside down to cool and level. Clean the mixing bowl.
3. To make the rose syrup, place the unrefined golden caster sugar and water in the mixing bowl. Cook **10 Min. / 120°C / Speed 1**. Add the rose water and combine **10 Sec. / Speed 2**. Pour half of the syrup into a small bowl and set aside. Brush the other half of the syrup over the cooled sponges.
4. Place 2 Tbsp of the leftover syrup back into the mixing bowl. Add the raspberries and icing sugar and mix **30 Sec. / Speed 4**. Pass through a fine mesh sieve into a bowl. Cover with cling film and set aside until later. Clean the mixing bowl.
5. Insert the butterfly whisk. Spoon the remaining leftover syrup into the mixing bowl and add the double cream. Whisk on **Speed 4** until stiff, watching carefully to avoid over-whipping (this could take anywhere from 20-45 seconds). Transfer to a bowl and chill until needed.
6. To assemble the cake, place one sponge on a plate, top with half the cream and decorate with 50g of the raspberries. Top with another cake base and repeat. Finally place the third cake base on top and drizzle over the rose raspberry icing. Smooth and leave to run down the sides. Decorate with rose petals and the remaining raspberries.

coffee & walnut cake

—A classic teatime treat

Coffee and walnut cake is the queen of all afternoon tea treats. I first came across it when I lived in Bristol and immediately fell in love with it. There is hardly any tea party without this classic. I quite like using instant espresso powder because it is easy and fast to dissolve, but you can also use freshly brewed espresso. Prepare the cake a day ahead and store in the fridge for up to three days.

**makes
16 slices**

280g unsalted butter, in small cubes
280g golden caster sugar (or caster sugar)
280g plain flour (or white spelt flour)
5 large eggs
1½ Tbsp baking powder
1 tsp vanilla extract
90g strong espresso, cold (or 1 ½ Tbsp
   instant espresso dissolved in 90g water)
100g walnut halves

250g unsalted butter, in small cubes
500g icing sugar
50g strong espresso, cold (or 1 Tbsp instant
   espresso dissolved in 50g water)
12 walnut halves

**prep:
2 hrs**

1. Preheat the oven to 180°C / 160°C Fan / Gas Mark 4. Line two 18cm round springform cake tins with greaseproof paper and set aside.
2. Place the butter in the mixing bowl. Blitz **40 sec. / Speed 5**. Scrape down using spatula.
3. Add the caster sugar, plain flour, eggs, baking powder, vanilla extract and espresso and combine **20 Sec. / Speed 5**. Scrape the mixture down using spatula, add the walnuts and combine again **3 Sec. / Speed 5**.
4. Divide the mixture evenly between the two cake tins and bake in the middle of the oven for 40-45 minutes until golden brown and a skewer inserted comes out clean. Remove and leave to cool for 5 minutes, then take the cakes out of the tins and place upside down on a wire cooling rack to cool. Clean the mixing bowl.
5. To make the buttercream, place the butter in the mixing bowl. Blitz **40 Sec. / Speed 5**. Scrape down using spatula. Insert the butterfly whisk. Mix **2 Min. / Speed 3.5**. Slowly insert the icing sugar through the hole in the mixing bowl lid using a tablespoon. Just before the time is up, add the espresso through the lid. Transfer a quarter of the mixture into a piping bag.
6. Using some of the buttercream from the mixing bowl, sandwich the two cooled sponges together. Then spread the remaining buttercream over the top and the sides to seal it. Pipe some icing around the rim of the cake and some in the centre and decorate with the walnut halves. Chill before serving.

Tip: You can easily prepare this cake by substituting the plain flour with gluten free plain flour, add 1 tsp xanthan gum and 75g whole milk.

macadamia brownies

—White chocolate and raspberry

Brownies are my speciality. Probably because they contain lots of chocolate and just look so delicious. I transformed my all-time favourite into something a little lighter here, and added some macadamia and pecan nuts for extra flavour and crunch. The raspberries add a little kick and make a gorgeous addition to your afternoon tea ceremony.

makes
16

200g dark chocolate, in small chunks
100g unsalted butter, in small cubes
200g caster sugar
4 large eggs
1 tsp vanilla extract
60g plain flour

60g cocoa powder
50g pecan nuts
50g macadamia nuts
200g white chocolate chips
150g fresh raspberries

prep:
50 min

1. Preheat the oven to 180°C / 160°C Fan / Gas Mark 4. Line a 20cm square baking tin with greaseproof paper and set aside.
2. Place the dark chocolate in the mixing bowl and chop **7 Sec. / Speed 9**. Scrape down using spatula, then melt **3 Min. / 37°C / Speed 1**.
3. Add the butter, caster sugar, eggs, vanilla extract, plain flour, cocoa powder, pecan nuts, macadamia nuts and white chocolate and mix **20 Sec. / Speed 4**. Pour the mixture into the prepared tin and decorate with the raspberries.
4. Bake in the oven for 35-40 minutes until deep brown and a skewer inserted comes out clean. If you prefer them a bit gooey, take them out after 30-35 minutes.
5. Transfer onto a wire cooling rack and leave to cool for 5 minutes before cutting into little squares. Store in a biscuit tin for up to 3 days.

apple & pecan cake

—A comforting treat for everyone

If you are thinking of throwing an autumn afternoon tea party, this American classic cannot be missed. It is filled with absolutely mouthwatering ingredients, such as apples, maple syrup and pecan nuts. This cake is both moist and fluffy and is just pure heaven on a plate!

makes
16 slices

100g pecan nuts

2 apples

150g unsalted butter

150g light soft brown sugar

100g maple syrup

1 tsp ground cinnamon

½ tsp vanilla extract

1 Tbsp baking powder

3 eggs

250g plain flour

20g maple syrup

prep:
1 hr

1. Preheat the oven to 180°C / 160°C Fan / Gas Mark 4. Line a 22cm round springform cake tin with greaseproof paper and set aside.
2. Place the pecans on a small rectangular baking tray and roast in the oven for 10 minutes. Tip into the mixing bowl and blitz **2 Sec. / Speed 4** until roughly chopped. Transfer to a small bowl and set aside.
3. Core and quarter the apples, leaving the skin on and chop into small pieces. Set aside.
4. Place the butter, light soft brown sugar, maple syrup, cinnamon, vanilla extract, baking powder, eggs and plain flour in the mixing bowl then mix **30 Sec. / Speed 5**. Add the apples and combine **30 Sec. / Reverse / Speed 3**. Pour into the prepared tin and top with the chopped pecan nuts.
5. Bake in the oven for 45 minutes (see tip).
6. Meanwhile, in a small saucepan melt the maple syrup over low heat. Remove the cake and brush over the maple syrup. Leave to cool in the tin for 5 minutes, then remove the tin and transfer onto a wire cooling rack. Leave to cool, then slice up!

Tip: For this recipe it is vital not to open the oven during the first 35 minutes of baking time, otherwise the centre of the cake will dip and you end up with some uncooked cake. If you feel like it is browning too quickly, turn down the heat to 170°C.

rhubarb cheesecake

—A baked version

During rhubarb season there are so many colourful recipes that you can try for afternoon tea but a cheesecake is definitely a good one for the list. I love baked cheesecake, having grown up with it in Germany, and think this rhubarb custard swirl adds such a great flavour to the original lemon cheesecake. Prepare it a day in advance and leave to set in the fridge for an even more intense flavour.

**makes
16 slices**

400g rhubarb, trimmed and cut into 2cm
   pieces
20g Grenadine (or pomegranate molasses)
50g golden caster sugar (or caster sugar)
2-3 drops natural pink food colouring
   (optional)
4 egg yolks
50g unsalted butter, in small cubes
20g cornflour

100g mascarpone
600g cream cheese
30g plain flour
150g golden caster sugar (or caster sugar)
2 lemons, zest
3 large eggs
2 egg yolks
100g sour cream

60g unsalted butter, in small cubes
200g digestive biscuits

**prep:
2 hrs**

1. Place the chopped rhubarb, Grenadine, sugar and pink food colouring (if using) in the mixing bowl. Cook **15 Min. / 90°C / Speed 1**. Scrape down any residue using a spatula, then pureé **30 Sec. / Speed 7** (don't leave Thermomix unattended while puréeing).

2. Add the egg yolks, unsalted butter and cornflour and cook **5 Min. / 90°C / Speed 3**. Pour onto a large plate and cover the top with cling film to avoid a skin from building. Leave to cool. Meanwhile, clean the mixing bowl.

3. Preheat the oven to 180°C / 160°C Fan / Gas Mark 4. Line a 22cm round springform cake tin with greaseproof paper.

4. Place the butter in the mixing bowl then melt **5 Min. / 55°C / Speed 1**. Add the digestive biscuits and crush **10 Sec. / Speed 8**. Transfer to the prepared tin and press down using the back of a spoon. Chill until later. Clean the mixing bowl again.

5. Place the mascarpone, cream cheese, plain flour, golden caster sugar, lemon zest, eggs, egg yolks and sour cream in the mixing bowl. Combine **30 Sec. / Speed 3**. Pour the mixture into the chilled tin and decorate with dollops of the cooled rhubarb custard. Bake in the oven for 50 minutes until golden and the middle is still a bit wobbly. Turn off the oven and leave to cool in there completely. Once cooled, after 3 hours, remove and chill before serving.

Tip: You can place the egg whites in a freezer bag, seal it and label with the date and the amount of egg whites. Store frozen for up to 3 months and defrost before using for pavlova or meringue.

sweet tarts & pastries

—*Almond Shortcrust Pastry*
—*Sweet Shortcrust Pastry*
—*Spelt Shortcrust Pastry*
—*Gluten Free Shortcrust Pastry*
—*Pimm's Cream Puffs*
—*Apricot Lavender Bites*
—*Coconut Tart*
—*Salted Caramel Eclairs*
—*Rhubarb Puff Tartlets*
—*Fresh Fig Tart*
—*Strawberry & Hibiscus Curd Tarts*
—*Lemon Mascarpone Tart*
—*Limoncello Mini Tarts*
—*Cherry Bakewell Tarts*
—*Raspberry Almond Tart*
—*Strawberry & Prosecco Tarts*
—*Jammy Jam Tarts*
—*Chocolate Mocha Tart*

pastry basics

almond shortcrust pastry

150g plain flour
50g ground almonds
100g unsalted butter, in small cubes
40g golden caster sugar
1 large egg

1. Place the plain flour, ground almonds, unsalted butter, golden caster sugar and egg in the mixing bowl. Combine **20 Sec. / Speed 6**.
2. Remove from the mixing bowl, form into a ball and use straight away.

sweet shortcrust pastry

200g plain flour or wholemeal flour
100g unsalted butter, in small cubes
40g golden caster sugar
1 large egg

1. Place the flour, unsalted butter, golden caster sugar and egg in the mixing bowl. Combine **20 Sec. / Speed 6**.
2. Remove from the mixing bowl, form into a ball and use straight away.

spelt shortcrust pastry

250g spelt flour (white or wholemeal)
100g unsalted butter, in small cubes
50g golden caster sugar
2 large egg yolks
20g water

1. Place the spelt flour, unsalted butter, caster sugar, egg yolks and water in the mixing bowl. Combine **20 Sec. / Speed 6**.
2. Remove from the mixing bowl, form into a ball and use straight away.

gluten free shortcrust pastry

175g gluten free plain flour
¼ tsp xanthan gum
40g unrefined golden caster sugar
75g unsalted butter, in small cubes
1 large egg

1. Place the gluten free plain flour, xanthan gum, sugar, butter and egg in the mixing bowl. Combine **20 Sec. / Speed 6**.
2. Remove from the mixing bowl, form into a ball and use straight away.

pimm's cream puffs

—Perfect for the tennis

When it is that time of the year for Wimbledon, the English take out their Pimm's and strawberries. I thought why not combine the love for cream puffs with that of all the goodies for the tennis, and I came up with these gorgeous Pimm's cream puffs. They are so lovely and fruity.

makes
20

150g water
80g unsalted butter, in small cubes
1 pinch sea salt
10g caster sugar
120g plain flour
3 large eggs

300g fresh strawberries
1 large orange

30g Pimm's
10g caster sugar
3-4 sprigs fresh mint

300g heavy whipping cream
50g Pimm's
10g caster sugar

icing sugar to dust

prep:
45 min

chill:
1 hr

1. Preheat the oven to 180°C / 160°C Fan / Gas Mark 4. Line two large rectangular baking trays with greaseproof paper and set aside.
2. Place the water, butter, salt and caster sugar in the mixing bowl. Melt **5 Min. / 100°C / Speed 1**. Add the plain flour and mix **20 Sec. / Speed 4**. Remove the lid and leave to cool for 10 minutes.
3. Mix again **1.5 Min. / Speed 5** while slowly cracking the eggs through the hole in the mixing bowl lid. Mix again **30 Sec. / Speed 5**.
4. Transfer the pastry mixture into a piping bag and cut off the bottom to make a small opening. Pipe little dollops onto the prepared trays, leaving some space in between each.
5. Bake in the oven for 20 minutes. Do not open the door during baking or the choux pastry can collapse. After 20 minutes, open the door and cut little slits in each choux bun then bake again for a further 3 minutes. Remove and leave to cool on a wire cooling rack.
6. To make the Pimm's infused fruit, cut the strawberries and oranges in small pieces and place in a large bowl. Cover with the Pimm's and sugar then refrigerate for 1 hour. Remove and sprinkle with the fresh mint.
7. To make the cream, insert the butterfly whisk. Place the cream in the mixing bowl and whisk on **Speed 4** until stiff, watching carefully to avoid over-whipping (this could take anywhere from 20-45 seconds). Transfer to a large bowl.
8. Halve each choux bun and fill with some cream and fruit. Top with the other half and dust with icing sugar. Refrigerate before serving.

apricot lavender bites

—White chocolate and raspberry

I love apricots. I could eat them all day and I love developing recipes including them. I've had such pleasure making these and they are so cute for the afternoon tea table. If you can get hold of fresh apricots, that is even better but canned work perfectly fine as well.

makes
12

40g plain flour
25g unsalted butter, in small cubes
35g caster sugar

200g plain flour
100g unsalted butter, in small cubes
40g caster sugar
1 egg

110g ground almonds
110g icing sugar
20g cornflour
110g unsalted butter, in small cubes
2 eggs
1 tsp vanilla extract

12 canned apricot halves

250g apricot jam (p. 41)
20g dried lavender

prep:
45 min

1. Preheat the oven to 180°C / 160°C Fan / Gas Mark 4. Grease a 12-hole cupcake tin with butter and set aside.
2. To make the crumble, place the plain flour, butter and sugar in the mixing bowl. Combine **5 Sec. / Speed 5**. Transfer into a small bowl and set aside. Without cleaning the mixing bowl, prepare the next step.
3. To make the pastry, place the plain flour, butter, caster sugar and egg in the mixing bowl. Blitz **20 Sec. / Speed 6**. Tip the pastry onto a floured surface and roll out to 1cm thickness. Cut out circles that fit the bottom of the cupcake tin. Place each circle into the prepared tin and set aside. Without cleaning the mixing bowl, prepare the next step.
4. To make the frangipane, place the ground almonds, icing sugar, cornflour, butter, eggs and vanilla extract in the mixing bowl. Combine **20 Sec. / Speed 4**. Transfer into a piping bag and cut off the bottom 4cm.
5. To assemble, drain and pat the apricot halves dry. Evenly divide the almond cream between the twelve holes, piping it on top of the pastry circles. Arrange an apricot half on top, with the cut side down and sprinkle with the crumble.
6. Bake in the oven for 25 minutes until golden brown.
7. To make the glaze, place the apricot jam and lavender in a small saucepan. Bring to the boil, then remove from the heat.
8. Remove the apricot frangipane bites from the oven and immediately brush with the apricot glaze. Drizzle with some lavender and leave to cool and set before removing from the tin.

coconut tart

—With passionfruit cream

Passionfruits are such a treat and so refreshing, especially in the summer. When you combine them with coconut, it makes a tropical tart that is too hard to resist. It reminds me of being on holidays.

makes
16 slices

200g plain flour
100g unsalted butter, in small cubes
40g golden caster sugar (or raw cane sugar)
1 egg

2 large eggs
1 lemon, zest and juice
100g maple syrup

250g double cream
200g desiccated coconut

200g crème fraîche (or Greek yoghurt)
300g heavy whipping cream
50g maple syrup
5 passionfruits, seeds and pulp scraped out

prep:
1 hr

1. Preheat the oven to 180°C / 160°C Fan / Gas Mark 4.
2. To make the pastry, place the plain flour, unsalted butter, caster sugar and egg in the mixing bowl. Blitz **20 Sec. / Speed 6**. Form into a ball, wrap in cling film and chill for 30 minutes.
3. Unwrap and roll out the pastry to ½cm thickness. Line a 24cm round loose bottom tin with the pastry and prick the base with a fork. Chill for 15 minutes.
4. Line the pastry with greaseproof paper and fill with baking beans. Bake for 15 minutes, then remove the beans and greaseproof paper and bake for a further 5 minutes. Meanwhile, clean the mixing bowl.
5. Place the eggs, lemon juice and zest, maple syrup, double cream and desiccated coconut in the mixing bowl. Combine **20 Sec. / Speed 4**. Pour over the baked tart case and bake again for 30-40 minutes until golden brown. Remove and transfer onto a wire cooling rack. Leave to cool. The coconut filling will set once cold. Clean the mixing bowl.
6. Insert the butterfly whisk and place the crème fraîche, heavy whipping cream and maple syrup in the mixing bowl. Whip **20 Sec. / Speed 4**. Add the passionfruit and combine **5 Sec. / Speed 4**. Pour over the cooled tart and spread all over. Chill before serving.

salted caramel éclairs

—With coffee filling

My partner Jesse loves coffee and éclairs so I have developed a recipe for him that combines both and makes them into an irresistible afternoon tea treat. These salted caramel éclairs are just so good, they cannot be missed when you are planning your tea party.

makes
12

150g water

80g unsalted butter, in small cubes

1 pinch sea salt

10g caster sugar

120g plain flour

3 large eggs

60g maple syrup

60g caster sugar

1 tsp vanilla extract

1 pinch sea salt

225g icing sugar

3 tsp instant coffee granules

50-100g water

300g heavy whipping cream

12 coffee beans

200g dark chocolate, in small chunks

prep:
1 hr

1. Preheat the oven to 180°C / 160°C Fan / Gas Mark 4. Line two large rectangular baking trays with greaseproof paper and set aside.

2. To make the pastry, place the water, butter, salt and caster sugar in the mixing bowl. Melt **5 Min./ 100°C / Speed 1**.

3. Add the plain flour and mix **20 Sec. / Speed 4**. Remove the lid and leave to cool for 10 minutes. Then mix again **1.5 Min. / Speed 5** while slowly cracking the eggs through the hole in the mixing bowl lid. Mix again **30 Sec. / Speed 5**.

4. Transfer the mixture into a piping bag and cut off the bottom to make a small opening. Pipe 7cm long sausages on the prepared trays, leaving some space in between because they will expand in the oven.

5. Bake in the oven for 20 minutes. Do not open the door during baking or the choux pastry can collapse. After 20 minutes, open the door and cut little slits in each éclair then bake again for a further 3 minutes.

6. To make the salted caramel filling, start by preparing the salted caramel. Place the maple syrup, sugar, vanilla extract and salt in the mixing bowl. Cook **5 Min. / Varoma / Speed 2 / no measuring cup**. Pour into a small bowl and leave to cool. Clean the mixing bowl.

7. To make the icing, place the icing sugar, instant coffee granules and 50g water in the mixing bowl then combine **20 Sec. / Speed 3** until it resembles thick custard. You may have to add more water depending on the consistency. Transfer into a bowl and cover with cling film. Set aside. Clean the mixing bowl again.

8. Once caramel is cool, insert the butterfly whisk and pour in the cream. Whisk on **Speed 4** until stiff, watching carefully to avoid over-whipping (this could take anywhere from 20-45 seconds). Carefully fold in the cooled caramel with your spatula and transfer the mixture into a piping bag fitted with a star nozzle.

9. Open each éclair and fill with some salted caramel cream, then close. Spread some of the icing on top and decorate with a coffee bean (optional).

10. To melt the chocolate, place it in the mixing bowl. Chop **7 Sec. / Speed 9**. Then melt **3 Min. / 37°C / Speed 1**. Pour into a piping bag and cut off only the tip and quickly drizzle over the eclairs. Leave to set before serving. Serve chilled.

rhubarb puff tartlets

—So fresh and light

These colourful little puff tarts are a great addition to a summery afternoon tea. You can make a large puff tart or individual mini tarts. They are refreshing and tangy.

makes
12 tarts

250g plain flour + extra for dusting
150g water
250g block of butter

180g cream cheese
30g caster sugar
2 tsp lemon juice

1 tsp vanilla extract

6 rhubarb stalks, trimmed
1 large egg
20g caster sugar
50g rhubarb jam (p. 43)

prep:
3 hrs

1. To make the pastry, place the plain flour and water in the mixing bowl. Mix **20 Sec. / Speed 6.** Transfer to a bowl and cover with cling film. Refrigerate for 2 hours. Wash mixing bowl.

2. Put the block of butter between two sheets of greaseproof paper. Using a rolling pin, roll it into a 15cm square, keeping the edges straight. Leave wrapped in the greaseproof paper and chill for 30 minutes.

3. On a lightly floured surface, roll out the chilled dough to a 30cm square. Place the butter on top at a 45° angle so that one edge of the butter is facing you. Fold over each corner of the dough to the centre to make a parcel. Use a pastry brush to brush off any flour. Press down the edges and flip upside down. Wrap in cling film and freeze for 10 minutes.

4. Once chilled, unwrap and roll out the dough to a rectangle of 20cm x 50cm. While rolling out, be gentle and do not press too hard, otherwise the butter will split. Fold the bottom third up, making sure that you keep brushing off the excess flour. Fold the top third down so that the dough is folded up like a letter. Wrap in cling film and freeze for 10 minutes. This is called a turn.

5. Remove from the freezer, unwrap and place the dough in front of you so that the folded edge is to your right. Repeat the same rolling out, folding, freezing process another three times.

6. Preheat the oven to 200°C / 180°C Fan / Gas Mark 6. Line two large rectangular baking trays with greaseproof paper and set aside.

7. Roll out the pastry into a long thin rectangle (approx. 20cm x 60cm). Cut out circles using an 11cm round cookie cutter or a small saucer. Place the circles on the trays, leaving a large gap in between each.

8. In a clean mixing bowl, place the cream cheese, caster sugar, lemon juice and vanilla extract and combine **20 Sec. / Speed 2.5.** Spread the mixture evenly over each circle, leaving a ½cm border. Cut the rhubarb into 6cm pieces and arrange on top of the cream cheese. Brush the borders of each puff tart with the egg and sprinkle each tart generously with caster sugar.

9. Bake in the oven for 20-25 minutes until golden brown and the rhubarb is soft. Transfer onto a wire cooling rack. While still hot, brush each tart with rhubarb jam and leave to cool before serving.

Tip: Prepare a couple of batches of puff pastry and freeze them in individual portions rolled out and rolled up on a piece of greaseproof paper wrapped in cling film. You can then thaw when needed and prepare gorgeous pastries in no time. Better than the shop-bought stuff!

fresh fig tart

—A Mediterranean treat

This is one of the quickest tarts you can whip up when throwing an afternoon tea party. Especially when figs are in season and you are lucky enough to have a fig tree at home – this is a great recipe to make use of those lovely fruits. You can also make mini tarts in cupcake tins, using one fig half per serving.

**makes
16 slices**

250g spelt flour (white or wholemeal)
100g unsalted butter, in small cubes
50g golden caster sugar
2 egg yolks
20g water

500g mascarpone cheese
60g honey
1 tsp vanilla extract
8 figs, halved

**prep:
2½ hrs**

1. Preheat the oven to 180°C / 160°C Fan / Gas Mark 4.
2. To make the pastry, place the spelt flour, unsalted butter, caster sugar, egg yolks and water in the mixing bowl. Combine **20 Sec. / Speed 6**. Transfer the pastry onto a floured surface and roll out to ½cm thickness. Line a 23cm round loose bottom pastry tin with the pastry and press down. Prick with a fork and chill for 15 minutes.
3. Line the pastry with greaseproof paper and fill with baking beans. Bake for 15 minutes, then remove the beans and greaseproof paper and bake for another 5 minutes. Meanwhile, clean the mixing bowl.
4. Place the mascarpone cheese, honey and vanilla extract in the mixing bowl and combine **30 Sec. / 37°C / Speed 3**. Pour over the tart shell and add the figs, cut side up. Bake for another 25-30 minutes until the tart is set but has a slight wobble to it. Leave to cool. Chill before serving.

strawberry & hibiscus curd tarts

—All those colours!

Curd is a great way to make a quick tart. Actually, this recipe could be prepared with any berry curd of your choice but I particularly love the added hibiscus which gives this strawberry curd a vibrant colour and tastes so delicious. This tart is gluten free and made with an almond crust. You could also use some hazelnuts or pecan nuts – or even mixed nuts – to make a lovely tart crust.

makes 6-8

240g golden caster sugar (or caster sugar)
30g hibiscus flowers, dried
3 limes, zest only
120g unsalted butter, in small cubes
3 large eggs
100g lime juice
100g fresh strawberries (or frozen, thawed)

150g almonds
50g gluten free plain flour
50g unsalted butter, in small cubes

40g golden caster sugar (or caster sugar)
1 egg

4 egg whites
2 tsp cream of tartar
200g golden caster sugar (or caster sugar)
1 tsp vanilla extract
2 tsp cornflour
a few drops pink food colouring (or gel colouring)

prep: 1 hr

chill: 1 hr

1. Preheat the oven to 180°C / 160°C Fan / Gas Mark 4.
2. Place the sugar and hibiscus flowers in the mixing bowl. Mill **15 Sec. / Speed 10**.
3. Add the lime zest and mill again **10 Sec. / Speed 10**. Add the butter, eggs, lime juice and strawberries then cook **20 Min. / 90°C / Speed 2 / no measuring cup**. Once cooked, place the measuring cup on the lid and blend **25 Sec. / Speed 6**. Pour into a large bowl and leave to cool. Meanwhile, clean the mixing bowl.
4. To make the pastry, place the whole almonds and gluten free plain flour in the mixing bowl. Mill **10 Sec. / Speed 10**. Add the butter, sugar and egg and combine **10 Sec. / Speed 6**. Divide the mixture between 6-8 mini 12cm loose bottom round tart tins and press down against the bottom and the edges with the back of a spoon (the pastry should be spreadable). Chill for 1 hour. Clean mixing bowl.
5. Line each pastry case with greaseproof paper and fill with baking beans. Bake for 15 minutes, then remove the beans and greaseproof paper and bake for a further 10 minutes until fully baked. Leave to cool.
6. Fill the pastry shell with the chilled strawberry-hibiscus curd and leave to set in the fridge for another 2 hours.
7. Insert the butterfly whisk. Place the egg whites and cream of tartar in the mixing bowl. Whisk **4 Min. / 37°C / Speed 3.5**. Whisk again **5 Min. / 37°C / Speed 3.5** and very slowly, every 20 seconds, add 1 Tbsp of the caster sugar through hole in the mixing bowl lid.
8. Add the vanilla extract and cornflour and whisk **1 Min. / Speed 3.5**.
9. Prepare your piping bag by using a wooden skewer to paint stripes of the food colouring down the inside of the bag. Fill it with the meringue, cut off the bottom 3cm and pipe little dollops onto each chilled tart. Serve chilled.

lemon mascarpone tart

—Like a light cheesecake

This lemon mascarpone tart is almost like a hybrid between a lemon tart and a lemon cheesecake. It is super light and has a very smooth finish. You can also add some blueberries on top to decorate.

**makes
16 slices**

175 gluten free plain flour
¼ tsp xanthan gum
40g raw cane sugar
75g unsalted butter, in small cubes
1 large egg

200g mascarpone
40g lemon juice
4 lemons, zest only
215g maple syrup
4 large eggs
4 large egg yolks (use whites for meringue)

**prep:
1 hr**

1. Preheat the oven to 180°C / 160°C Fan / Gas Mark 4.
2. To make the pastry, place the gluten free plain flour, xanthan gum, sugar, butter and egg in the mixing bowl. Combine **20 Sec. / Speed 6**. Form into a ball, wrap in cling film and chill for 15 minutes.
3. Unwrap and roll out the pastry to ½cm thickness. Line a 24cm round loose bottom tin with the pastry and prick the base with a fork. Chill for 15 minutes.
4. Line the pastry with greaseproof paper and fill with baking beans. Bake for 15 minutes, then remove the beans and greaseproof paper and bake for another 5 minutes. Meanwhile, clean the mixing bowl.
5. Place the mascarpone, lemon juice and zest and maple syrup in the mixing bowl. Combine **20 Sec. / Speed 4**. Transfer to a small bowl and set aside. Clean the mixing bowl again.
6. Insert the butterfly whisk and crack in the eggs and egg yolks. Whisk **6 Min. / 37°C / Speed 4**. Mix again **6 Min. / Speed 4**. Add the mascarpone mixture and combine **4 Sec. / Speed 3**. Transfer into the baked tart case and bake for 25-35 minutes until the mixture is set but still a little wobbly. Remove from the oven and transfer onto a wire cooling rack. Leave to cool. The mixture will set once cooled.

Tip: This cheesecake is also really tasty with spelt crust. Follow the recipe on p. 99 for the pastry.

limoncello mini tarts

—A boozy and zingy teatime treat

Lemon meringue pie is a classic afternoon tea treat. This boozy version is made with limoncello and is a superb adult tart for a birthday party or a special occasion. You can also make a large tart by using a 23cm fluted tin and pipe little dollops or roses on each tart. It is best served fresh and chilled.

makes
12

100g plain flour + extra for dusting
100g wholemeal flour
100g unsalted butter, in small cubes + extra
   for greasing
40g golden caster sugar (or caster sugar)
1 egg

4 egg whites
2 tsp cream of tartar
200g golden caster sugar (or caster sugar)
1 tsp vanilla extract
2 tsp cornflour

300g limoncello curd (p. 40)

prep:
1 hr

1. Preheat the oven to 180°C / 160°C Fan / Gas Mark 4. Grease a 12-hole muffin tin with butter and dust with flour or use a non-stick tin.
2. To make the pastry, place the plain flour, wholemeal flour, unsalted butter, caster sugar and egg in the mixing bowl. Blitz **20 Sec. / Speed 6**. Form into a ball, wrap in cling film and chill for 30 minutes.
3. Unwrap and roll out the pastry to ½cm thickness. Cut out 12 rounds with a 9cm cookie cutter. Place in the muffin tin and press down slightly. Chill for 15 minutes.
4. Line each pastry case with greaseproof paper and fill with baking beans. Bake for 15 minutes, then remove the beans and greaseproof paper and bake for another 10 minutes until baked fully. Remove and leave to cool. Clean the mixing bowl.
5. Insert the butterfly whisk and place the egg whites and cream of tartar in the mixing bowl. Whisk **4 Min. / 37°C / Speed 3.5**. Whisk again **5 Min. / 37°C / Speed 3.5** and very slowly, every 20 seconds, add 1 Tbsp of the caster sugar through hole in the mixing bowl lid.
6. Add the vanilla extract and cornflour and whisk **1 Min. / Speed 3**. Spoon the mixture into a piping bag.
7. Spoon some limoncello curd into each pastry case and pipe with some meringue. Use a blow-torch to toast the meringue lightly and serve. You can also serve them chilled.

cherry bakewell tarts

—With an almond crust

Cherry Bakewell tarts are probably the best afternoon tea tarts you could ever think of. I've used morello cherry jam to make them extra tasty and decorated them with some flaked almonds for a lovely finish. If you prefer a gluten free or wheat free base, check out my basic pastry recipes at the beginning of the chapter.

makes
12

200g plain flour
100g unsalted butter, in small cubes
40g golden caster sugar (or caster sugar)
1 egg

50g unsalted butter, in small cubes
50g golden caster sugar (or caster sugar)
1 egg
1 egg yolk
1 tsp vanilla extract
50g ground almonds
20g plain flour

30g morello cherry jam
50g flaked almonds
12 glacé cherries

100g icing sugar
½ tsp almond extract

prep:
1 hr

1. Preheat the oven to 180°C / 160°C Fan / Gas Mark 4. Grease a 12-hole muffin tin with butter and dust with flour or use a non-stick tin.
2. To make the pastry, place the plain flour, unsalted butter, caster sugar and egg in the mixing bowl. Blitz **20 Sec. / Speed 6**.
3. Transfer the pastry onto a floured surface and roll out to ½cm thickness. Cut out 12 rounds with a 9cm cookie cutter. Place in the muffin tin and press down slightly. Chill for 15 minutes. Clean the mixing bowl.
4. To make the frangipane, place the unsalted butter, caster sugar, egg, egg yolk, vanilla extract, ground almonds and plain flour in the mixing bowl. Combine **20 Sec. / Speed 4**. Transfer into a small bowl and set aside.
5. Remove the pastry tin from the fridge, place ½ tsp cherry jam in each pastry shell and top off with the frangipane so that they are half full. Bake in the oven for 25 minutes. Remove tarts from the oven and from the cupcake tin. Leave to cool on a wire cooling rack.
6. Toast the almond flakes in the oven for 3-4 minutes. Transfer into a small bowl and leave to cool. Once cool, place the icing sugar and almond extract in a small bowl and add enough water to make a thick paste. Spread over the tarts and top off with one glacé cherry. Decorate with flaked almonds around the edge of each tart.

raspberry almond tart

—Fluffy frangipane

This is probably the best frangipane I have ever eaten. Whether you prepare this gorgeous raspberry almond tart in a rectangular or round tart tin, it is definitely a showstopper for your afternoon tea table.

250g spelt flour (white or wholemeal)
100g unsalted butter, in small cubes
50g golden caster sugar (or caster sugar)
2 egg yolks
20g water

200g unsalted butter, in small cubes
200g ground almonds
3 large eggs
200g maple syrup

40g apricot jam
400g fresh raspberries
icing sugar to dust

prep:
2½ hrs

1. Place the spelt flour, unsalted butter, caster sugar, egg yolks and water in the mixing bowl. Combine **20 Sec. / Speed 6**. Transfer onto a floured surface and roll out to ½cm thickness. Line a 36 x 12cm rectangular or 23cm round loose bottom pastry tin with the pastry and press down. Prick with a fork and chill for 15 minutes.
2. Preheat the oven to 180°C / 160°C Fan / Gas Mark 4.
3. Line the pastry with greaseproof paper and fill with baking beans. Bake for 15 minutes, then remove the beans and greaseproof paper and bake for a further 5 minutes. Meanwhile, clean the mixing bowl.
4. Place the unsalted butter, ground almonds, eggs and maple syrup in the mixing bowl and combine **30 Sec. / Speed 4**.
5. Remove the tart from the oven and pour over the frangipane. Spread evenly and bake for another 30 minutes. Leave to cool on a wire cooling rack.
6. Warm the apricot jam in a small saucepan over medium heat until bubbling. Brush over the cooled frangipane and decorate with raspberries. Dust with icing sugar.

Tip: If you don't have ceramic baking beans, simply use dried kidney beans or peas.

strawberry & prosecco tarts

—With an almond crust

Aren't these strawberry Prosecco tarts just perfect? It is like afternoon tea and champagne in one. The almond crust makes them extra delicious and super crunchy. If you have children around, you can either use alcohol-free Prosecco or substitute with milk.

makes
6 tarts

150g plain flour
50g ground almonds
100g unsalted butter, in small cubes
40g golden caster sugar (or caster sugar)
1 egg

375g whole milk
125g Prosecco
1 vanilla pod, seeds scraped
50g golden caster sugar (or caster sugar)

4 egg yolks (use the whites to make meringue)
40g cornflour
40g unsalted butter, in small cubes
250g whipping cream
250g double cream (or thickened cream)

400g strawberries
150g apricot jam (p. 41)

prep:
2 hrs

1. Preheat the oven to 180°C / 160°C Fan / Gas Mark 4.
2. To make the pastry, place the plain flour, ground almonds, unsalted butter, caster sugar and egg in the mixing bowl. Blitz **20 Sec. / Speed 6**.
3. Transfer the pastry onto a floured surface and divide into six balls. Roll each out to ½cm thickness. Line six mini 12cm loose bottom fluted tart tins with the pastry and prick the base with a fork. Chill for 15 minutes.
4. Line each pastry case with greaseproof paper and fill with baking beans. Bake for 15 minutes, then remove the beans and greaseproof paper and bake for a further 5 minutes. The pastry cases should be fully baked. Leave to cool. Meanwhile, clean the mixing bowl.
5. Place the milk, prosecco, vanilla pod, sugar, egg yolks, cornflour and butter in the mixing bowl. Warm **9 Min. / 90°C / Speed 3**. Transfer to a large bowl and cover the top with cling film to avoid a skin from forming. Leave to set and cool for at least 1 hour. Clean the mixing bowl.
6. Place the cooled crème pâtissière back in the mixing bowl and blitz **20 sec. / Speed 3** to smooth it. Pour in a large bowl and set aside. Clean the mixing bowl.
7. Insert the butterfly whisk. Pour in the whipping cream and double cream. Whisk on **Speed 4** until stiff, watching carefully to avoid over-whipping (this could take anywhere from 20-45 seconds). Transfer into the bowl with the crème pâtissière. Combine with a whisk until fluffy.
8. Once cooled, fill each pastry case with the champagne cream and chill for 15 minutes.
9. Quarter the strawberries and arrange on top of the crème pâtissière. Warm the apricot jam over a low heat in a small saucepan. Using a pastry brush, glaze the strawberries and leave to harden before serving.

jammy jam tarts

—Lemon, orange & raspberry

Jammy jam tarts are so simple to prepare and always a hit for afternoon tea. You can fill the pastry shells with any jam you like – delicious.

makes
12

250g spelt flour (white or wholemeal)
100g unsalted butter, in small cubes
50g golden caster sugar
2 egg yolks
20g water

2 Tbsp lemon curd
2 Tbsp orange marmalade, thick cut
2 Tbsp strawberry jam

prep:
45 min

1. Preheat the oven to 180°C / 160°C Fan / Gas Mark 4. Grease a 12-hole muffin tin with butter and dust with flour or use a non-stick tin.

2. Place the spelt flour, unsalted butter, caster sugar, egg yolks and water in the mixing bowl. Combine **20 Sec. / Speed 6**. Tip the pastry onto a floured surface.

3. Roll out the pastry to ½cm thickness. Cut out 12 rounds with a 9cm fluted cookie cutter. Place in the muffin tin and press down slightly. Chill for 15 minutes.

4. Add 1 tsp jam or curd to each pastry case and bake for 15-20 minutes until lightly brown and the jam is bubbling. Remove and leave to cool. The jam will set once cooled.

Tip: You can freeze these jam tarts cooked and defrost before use. They last in the freezer for up to 3 months.

chocolate mocha tart

—Simply stunning

How would you feel about combining your love of chocolate with your addiction to coffee? I have found you a new favourite tart then! This is the best chocolate mocha tart ever and it contains a chocolatey pastry topped with the world's creamiest mocha mousse. So tasty. I topped it with some freeze-dried raspberries and cacao nibs for the ultimate finish.

makes
16 slices

180g plain flour
20g cocoa powder
100g unsalted butter, in small cubes
50g golden caster sugar
1 egg

50g golden caster sugar
1 tsp instant espresso (or 2 tsp instant coffee)

200g dark chocolate, in small chunks
60g double cream (or thickened cream)
4 eggs

20g freeze-dried fruit (optional)
10g cacao nibs

prep:
1 hr

chill:
3 hrs

1. Preheat the oven to 180°C / 160°C Fan / Gas Mark 4.
2. To make the pastry, place the plain flour, cocoa powder, unsalted butter, caster sugar and egg in the mixing bowl. Blitz **20 Sec. / Speed 6**. Form into a ball and roll out the pastry to ½cm thickness. Line a 24cm round loose bottom tin with the pastry and prick the base with a fork. Chill for 15 minutes.
3. Line the pastry with greaseproof paper and fill with baking beans. Bake for 15 minutes, then remove the beans and greaseproof paper and bake for a further 10 minutes until baked fully. Remove and leave to cool. Meanwhile, clean the mixing bowl.
4. Place the caster sugar in the mixing bowl. Blitz **10 Sec. / Speed 10**. Add the instant espresso and chocolate and blitz **3 Sec. / Speed 9**. Add the cream and melt **4 Min. / 50°C / Speed 2**. Separate the eggs, place the egg whites in a small bowl and add the egg yolks to the melted chocolate. Combine **15 Sec. / Speed 4**. Transfer to a large metal bowl and set aside. Clean the mixing bowl (it needs to be completely grease-free).
5. Insert the butterfly whisk. Add the reserved egg whites and whisk **3 Min. / Speed 3.5**. Pour the egg whites into the chocolate mixture and fold in using a large whisk. Pour the mixture (it should be thick but still runny) over the cooled tart case and chill for at least 3 hours before serving. Decorate with freeze-dried fruit and cacao nibs. Serve chilled.

cookies & biscuits

jammie dodgers

—Chocolate mint

Jammie Dodgers are so tasty and recently I have been thinking about different flavour combinations. I finally found something I really liked and it involves chocolate. They are so yummy and make a beautiful addition to your afternoon tea party.

makes
24

125g unsalted butter, in small cubes
150g raw cane sugar
1 tsp vanilla extract
1 large egg
200g plain flour
50g cocoa powder

200g unsalted butter, in small cubes
400g icing sugar
15g water
½ tsp peppermint extract
200g blackcurrant jam

prep:
1 hr

1. Preheat the oven to 180°C / 160°C Fan / Gas Mark 4. Line two large rectangular baking trays with greaseproof paper and set aside.
2. Place the butter, sugar, vanilla extract, egg, plain flour and cocoa powder in the mixing bowl. Combine **20 Sec. / Speed 6**.
3. Transfer onto a floured surface and roll out to ½cm thickness. Using a Jammie Dodger cookie cutter, cut out equal numbers of cookies with and without a jam hole. You can reshape and re-roll the cookie dough as many times as necessary. Transfer the cookies onto prepared baking trays then bake for 10-12 minutes until light browned. Transfer onto a wire cooling rack and leave to cool. Clean the mixing bowl.
4. To make the buttercream, place the butter in the mixing bowl. Soften **40 Sec. / Speed 5**. Insert the butterfly whisk. Whisk **2 Min. / Speed 3.5** while adding the icing sugar through the hole in mixing bowl lid. During the last 20 seconds, slowly add in the water and peppermint extract. Transfer the mixture into a piping bag and cut off the bottom 2cm.
5. To assemble the Jammie Dodgers, pipe a few dollops of the buttercream on each whole cookie, spoon a little jam on top and top with a cookie with a hole. Repeat until used up. Store in a biscuit tin for up to 4 weeks.

tahini cookies

—Gluten free pleasure

These tahini cookies are so moist and the perfect addition to a Mediterranean themed afternoon tea. You could combine them with a fragrant rose cake and the fig tart for a great tea party menu.

makes
18

140g ground almonds
1 tsp baking powder
150g maple syrup
100g tahini
½ tsp vanilla extract
20 whole almonds

prep:
25 min

1. Preheat the oven to 180°C / 160°C Fan / Gas Mark 4. Line a large rectangular baking tray with greaseproof paper and set aside.
2. Place the ground almonds, baking powder, maple syrup, tahini and vanilla extract in the mixing bowl. Combine **20 Sec. / Speed 4**. Place teaspoons of the mixture onto the prepared tray and press down slightly with a fork. Decorate with an almond piece and bake in the oven for 10-15 minutes until lightly golden.
3. Remove and transfer onto a wire cooling rack. Leave to cool and harden before serving.

ginger custard creams

—So creamy

Oh heavens, custard creams. They have got to be one of my all-time favourite biscuits. I don't think you can really afford to miss them on your afternoon tea table but if you don't like the sound of ginger, simply leave it out to make standard custard creams.

makes
24

200g unsalted butter, in small cubes
125g icing sugar
1 tsp vanilla extract
2 large eggs
325g plain flour
25g cornflour
½ tsp baking powder

2 tsp ground ginger
¼ tsp ground cinnamon

200g unsalted butter, in small cubes
400g icing sugar
1 tsp ground ginger
15g water

prep:
1½ hrs

1. Preheat the oven to 180°C / 160°C Fan / Gas Mark 4. Line two large rectangular trays with greaseproof paper and set aside.
2. Place the butter, icing sugar, vanilla extract, eggs, plain flour, cornflour, baking powder, ground ginger and ground cinnamon in the mixing bowl. Combine **20 Sec. / Speed 6**.
3. Transfer onto a floured surface and roll out to 0.5cm thickness. Using a rectangular cookie cutter and a custard cream cookie stamp (optional), cut out as many biscuits as you can until you have used up all the cookie dough. You can reshape and re-roll the dough as needed. Place on the prepared trays and refrigerate for 15 minutes.
4. Then bake for 10-12 minutes until lightly browned. Remove and transfer onto a wire cooling rack. Leave to cool. Meanwhile, clean the mixing bowl.
5. To make the buttercream, place the butter in the mixing bowl. Soften **40 Sec. / Speed 5**. Insert the butterfly whisk. Whisk **2 Min. / Speed 3.5** while adding the icing sugar and ground ginger through the hole in mixing bowl lid. During the last 20 seconds, slowly add in the water. Transfer the mixture into a piping bag and cut off the bottom 3cm.
6. Pipe half the cookies with some buttercream and sandwich with the other half. Leave to harden before serving. You can store them in a biscuit tin for up to 4 weeks.

passionfruit jaffa cakes

—Perfect for the summer

Jaffa cakes have been around since my childhood and I remember back home in Germany I used to get them with raspberry flavour and in the summertime they had a special edition which was made with passionfruit and mango. I have recreated this recipe and am very pleased with the results. These jaffa cakes are quite large but perfect for afternoon tea.

makes
12

10g gelatine leaves (or 15g gelatine powder)
30g caster sugar
250g fresh mango juice
7 passionfruit

50g caster sugar
½ tsp vanilla extract
50g plain flour
1 tsp baking powder

butter for greasing
2 eggs

200g dark chocolate

prep:
1½ hr

chill:
2 hrs

1. Place the gelatine leaves and sugar in the mixing bowl (If you are using powder, you can skip this step). Blitz **20 Sec. / Speed 10**. Scrape down using your spatula.
2. Add the mango juice and scrape out the seeds and pulp of the passionfruit into the mixing bowl. Blitz **5 Sec. / Speed 5**. Then warm **5 Min. / 80°C / Speed 2**. Meanwhile, line a 20cm square tin with cling film.
3. Once the passionfruit jelly is cooked, pass it through a fine sieve into the prepared tin and leave to set at room temperature for 1 hour. Then refrigerate for at least 2 hours or overnight.
4. To make the sponge, preheat the oven to 180°C / 160°C Fan / Gas Mark 4. Grease a 12-hole muffin tin or a small bun tin with butter and set aside.
5. Insert the butterfly whisk. Place the eggs, caster sugar and vanilla extract in the mixing bowl. Whisk **3 Min. / 37°C / Speed 4**. Mix again **3 Min. / Speed 4** (no temperature). Add the plain flour and baking powder and combine **4 Sec. / Speed 3**. Pour level tablespoons of the mixture into the prepared muffin tray in each hole. Bake in the oven for 10 minutes until lightly golden. Carefully tip the muffin tray over onto a wire cooling rack, releasing the cakes immediately. Leave to cool. Remove the jelly from the fridge and lift out of the tin. Cut out little circles or hearts or whatever
6. you feel looks cute, each just smaller than the cakes. Place them on top of the cooled cakes. To melt the chocolate, place the dark chocolate in the mixing bowl and blitz **5 Sec. / Speed 9**.
7. Scrape down using spatula. Melt **3 Min. / 37°C / Speed 2**. Lay a piece of greaseproof paper underneath the cooling rack with the Jaffa cakes. Pour the melted chocolate over the jelly. The chocolate will drip onto the greaseproof paper and
8. it makes it easier to discard later. Leave to set before serving.

Tip: You can also use orange juice if you want. Just choose your favourite flavour.

pecan shortbread

—Gluten and guilt free

This is the best shortbread if you are looking for something full of flavour and gluten free. They are the perfect snack size and make a beautiful addition to your afternoon tea menu. They store really well in a biscuit tin and you could even coat them in a bit of vegan chocolate.

makes
24

50g pecan nuts
200g coconut oil
1 ripe banana, halved
150g raw cane sugar
300g gluten free plain flour
1 tsp vanilla extract
1 pinch sea salt
1 tsp xanthan gum

prep:
45 min

1. Preheat the oven to 180°C / 160°C Fan / Gas Mark 4. Line two large rectangular baking trays with greaseproof paper.
2. Place the pecans in the mixing bowl. Blitz **2 Sec. / Speed 5**. Add the coconut oil, banana, sugar, flour, vanilla extract, salt and xanthan gum and combine **20 Sec. / Speed 6**.
3. Pour the mixture onto a floured surface and divide in half. Shape each half into a sausage shape approx. 5cm diameter and wrap in cling film individually. Freeze for at least 20 minutes. You can at this stage also freeze them for up to three months for later use.
4. Remove the log from the freezer and unwrap. Cut into 1 cm thick circles. Place on the prepared trays and bake in the oven for 10-15 minutes until lightly golden. Remove and leave to cool on a wire cooling rack before serving. You can store them in a biscuit tin for up to four weeks.

chocolate biscotti

—So chocolatey

These double chocolate biscotti are very special. They are perfect with a cup of Earl Grey tea and best served with some coffee éclairs and strawberry tarts for the ultimate afternoon tea indulgence.

makes
24

100g almonds
100g unsalted butter, in small cubes
3 large eggs
200g caster sugar
1 tsp vanilla extract
325g plain flour

2 tsp baking powder
1 pinch sea salt flakes
40g cocoa powder
100g dark chocolate chips

200g dark chocolate (minimum 70%)

prep:
4 hrs

1. Preheat the oven to 180°C / 160°C Fan / Gas Mark 4. Line two large rectangular baking trays with greaseproof paper and set aside.
2. Place the almonds in the mixing bowl. Blitz **2 Sec. / Speed 4**. Transfer into a small bowl and set aside.
3. Add the butter to the mixing bowl. Melt **3 Min. / 55°C / Speed 1**. Add the chopped almonds, eggs, sugar, vanilla extract, flour, baking powder, salt, cocoa powder and chocolate chips and combine **20 Sec. / Speed 6**. The mixture will be very stiff so you might have to help with your spatula through hole in the mixing bowl lid.
4. Divide the mixture between the two trays and dust your hands with flour. Shape each piece of dough into a long log (approx. 23cm long and 7cm wide). Bake each in the oven for 25-30 minutes. Remove and transfer onto a wire cooling rack. Leave to cool until completely cold.
5. When they are cold, cut them into long pieces diagonally, approx. 1cm thick. Preheat the oven to 180°C / 160°C Fan / Gas Mark 4. Place the biscotti pieces on the baking trays again and bake for another 10-15 minutes until hardened. Remove and leave to cool.
6. Place the dark chocolate in the mixing bowl. Chop **7 Sec. / Speed 9** then melt **3 Min. / 37°C / Speed 1**. Transfer to a small bowl and dip each cooled biscotti in the chocolate. Leave to harden before serving. They store well in a biscuit tin for up to 4 weeks.

peanut butter cookies

—With banana and chocolate

Peanut butter cookies are a classic. These ones are made with spelt flour for some extra flavour, and I have added bananas and chocolate chips for some additional aromas. You can prepare them in advance and freeze them, too.

makes
12

70g unsalted butter
2 ripe bananas, halved
100g crunchy peanut butter
135g raw cane sugar
1 tsp vanilla extract
200g spelt flour
1 Tbsp baking powder
200g dark chocolate chips

prep:
20 min

1. Preheat the oven to 180°C / 160°C Fan / Gas Mark 4. Line a large rectangular baking tray with greaseproof paper and set aside.
2. Place the butter in the mixing bowl. Melt **3 Min. / 55°C / Speed 1**.
3. Add the bananas, peanut butter, sugar, vanilla extract, spelt flour and baking powder to the mixing bowl. Combine **20 Sec. / Speed 4**.
4. Add the chocolate chips and fold in with your spatula. Place teaspoons of the mixture onto the prepared trays, pressing them down slightly.
5. Bake for 10-12 minutes until lightly browned. Remove and transfer onto a wire cooling rack. Leave to cool before serving. You can store the cookies in a biscuit tin for up to 4 weeks.

lavender shortbread

—So aromatic

These lavender shortbread are so fragrant, the whole house will be filled with the smell of fresh lavender when you are baking them. They are the ideal teatime biscuit and make such a gorgeous addition to your afternoon tea tray. You can store them in a biscuit tin for up to four weeks.

makes
24

175g cold unsalted butter, in small cubes
100g caster sugar
225g plain flour
2 Tbsp dried lavender

prep:
30 min

1. Preheat the oven to 180°C / 160°C Fan / Gas Mark 4. Line two large rectangular baking trays with greaseproof paper and set aside.
2. Place the butter, sugar and plain flour in the mixing bowl. Blitz **20 Sec. / Speed 6**. Transfer the mixture onto a floured surface and add the lavender, working it in using your hands. Then roll out the cookie dough into a 1cm thick rectangle. Cut out rectangles using a cookie cutter. You can also use a cookie stamp to make a shortbread pattern, or use heart shapes.
3. Place the cookies onto the prepared trays and refrigerate for 10 minutes. Then bake for 10-15 minutes until lightly golden. Transfer onto a wire cooling rack and leave to cool.

Tip: Instead of plain flour you can also use gluten free plain flour and add 1 tsp xanthan gum to the mixture or for a more wholesome treat add some wholemeal flour or spelt flour.

F NE

cardamom biscuits

—So fragrant

These cardamom biscuits are perfect with a strong cup of tea. I would serve them with Assam or Masala tea alongside other fragrant treats. I love them and think they are so adorable. You can cut out any shapes you like.

makes
24

300g wholemeal plain flour
125g caster sugar
½ tsp ground cardamom
200g unsalted butter, in small cubes
2 tsp vanilla extract
24 blanched hazelnuts

prep:
25 min

1. Preheat the oven to 180°C / 160°C Fan / Gas Mark 4. Line two large rectangular baking trays with greaseproof paper and set aside.
2. Place the flour, sugar, cardamom, butter and vanilla extract in the mixing bowl. Combine **20 Sec. / Speed 6**.
3. Tip onto a floured surface and roll out to 1cm thickness. Cut out little hearts with a cookie cutter and transfer onto the prepared trays. Decorate each cookie with a hazelnut and press in lightly. Bake for 10-12 minutes until lightly brown.
4. Remove and transfer onto a wire cooling rack. Leave to cool before serving. You can store the cookies in a biscuit tin for up to 4 weeks.

index

HOMEBAKED

ThermoMix. Bake. Eat. Repeat.

by Sophia Handschuh
www.thermomixbakingblogger.com

Nothing says home like the smell of baking. In this book you will find simple and reliable recipes that make you a Thermomix star baker. Unleash your inner superpowers with these ultimate tips and guides to Thermomix baking. From bread to choux pastry, this book is your perfect baking companion. All you need is a few hungry people. So let's get baking, shall we?

A fantastic all-round Thermomix book by the author of *Homebaked*, Sophia Handschuh, award-winning blogger ranked in the Top 15 for baking blogs on the web.

Supercharged

Delicious Thermomix recipes to kickstart a healthy routine

Sophia Handschuh
thermomixbakingblogger.com

Supercharged is a stunning recipe collection packed with refreshing recipes to kickstart a healthier baking routine. After the success of her bestselling books, Sophia has thought of a new way to keep you busy with your Thermomix. This recipe collection contains recipes that are gluten free, vegan, sugar free and will help you tackle new types of baking one tasty recipe at a time.

notes

acknowledgements

At the beginning of every new book project I feel so overwhelmed by the all of the stages ahead of me. Luckily, I have the most supportive partner you could ever imagine. I would like to express a huge thank you to Jesse who is always here when I need him. After long days of work he always came home and helped with the cleaning when I created chaos in the kitchen during the recipe development stage. Right from the beginning, he always makes sure I keep sane and don't get overwhelmed and overworked. I could not do this job without him. Thank you Jesse for being so amazing.

I would like to thank my mum who actually inspired me to write this book. I have dedicated it to her because I think she is the biggest afternoon tea fan I have ever known and during her birthday celebrations we had the glorious idea to turn her obsession and my passion into this amazing book project. Thank you mum for supporting me and inspiring me. And of course I would like to thank my dad without whom I would never have been here now. I am so glad to have such supporting parents who keep believing in me even when I have moments of doubt.

No book is done only by one person. There are so many parties involved, like the printer, the copy editor, the recipe testers and designers and the author. I have actually accumulated a little team this time and must say it made life so much easier.

First of all, thank you to Emma Buckley, my copy editor, who has done an outstanding job at detecting even the smallest mistakes in this book. You helped me achieve such a professional standard for this book and showed such initiative to making the flow of this book so smooth and lovely. I hope to continue working on many more exciting projects with you.

I would also like to thank all the lovely recipe testers who have taken time of their personal life to try out the recipes in this book. It has truly made a difference to the quality of the recipes and I am so glad you all agreed to take part in the development of this book. You are all a part of this and I could not have achieved such perfection without you.

This is the third book launch and finally I can thank a professional layout designer for a beautiful result. Anna Green, you have really inspired the style of this book and made it a true masterpiece. Thank you for your flexibility, attention to detail and superb design work. I think I am not the only one who would say this is the best book so far. You've taken it to the next level.

All these wonderful people have made this project a true success for me and I am so excited that the end result is so amazing. I cannot wait to see what the future will hold for us and 'Team Sophia'.